Crochet
Yourself Calm

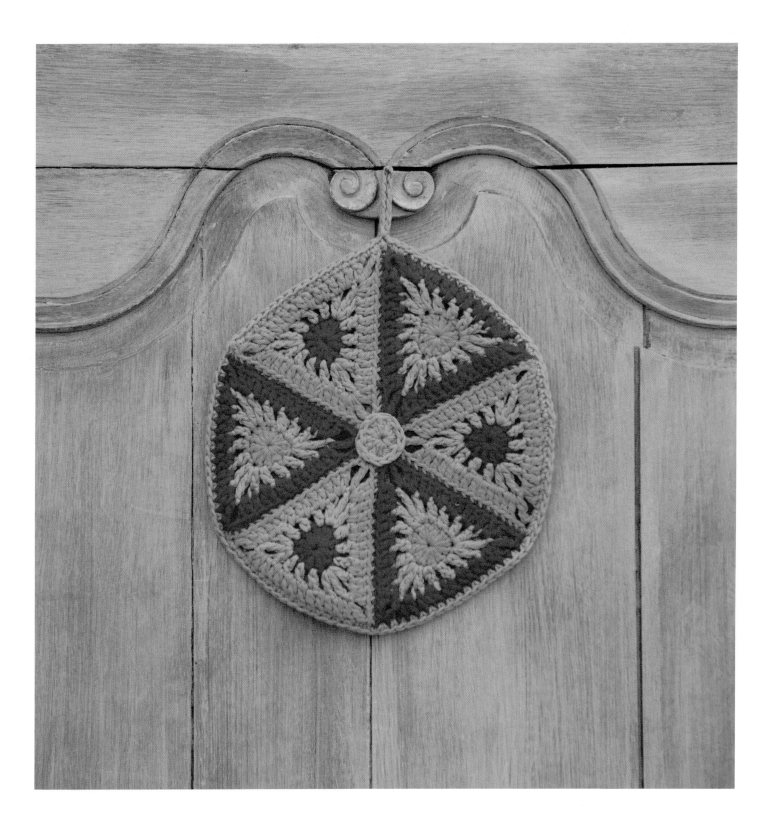

Crochet
Yourself Calm

CARMEN HEFFERNAN

LARK
New York

Introduction

Crochet brings me great peace and joy, and it can for you, too. When you are focusing on the repetitive rhythms of creating your piece, stitch-by-stitch, you are truly in the moment and more mindful: Your breathing and heart rate slows down, your serotonin levels rise, and you become calm.

The act of creating is known to have a healing effect on the mind, which is harnessed by art therapists. Add the impact of other therapies involved in crochet— color and touch—along with the spiritual significance of many of the geometric shapes, and crochet becomes a powerful tool in reducing stress and increasing feelings of well-being. Plus, you will have made a beautiful, one-of-a-kind piece.

Everyone's idea of calm is different, and crochet embraces them all. I am inspired by the dramatic light and landscape of my native Ireland, and find striking color combinations relaxing; but you may prefer to create a more traditionally calming effect in cooler colors. I find the feel of the yarn soothing, too, as is the range of textures you can create, from delicate, open lace to textiles with a raised surface.

I hope you enjoy making the motifs and patterns in this book, and have fun creating the projects. I also hope that, like me, you will benefit from the wonderful peace of mind that comes from being lost in the creative process, and that this enriches other areas of your life in the most surprising and joyful ways.

Carmen Heffernan

CARMEN HEFFERNAN

Contents

Circles

Circular motifs create restful ripples of color, which radiate from the center of the design. Assemble a group of these shapes to create a shawl that resembles a field of flowers or use a mandala to decorate a wall or table, or embellish a shopping basket.

EMBELLISHED BASKET
Transform a simple shopping basket into a designer accessory by decorating it with a crocheted mandala. The result will turn heads wherever you go and ensure that your shopping always travels in style. For the instructions to make this design, see page 14.

Cluster Circle

A circle of crochet stitches gives first-time crocheters the chance to get comfortable working in rounds with single and double crochet, making stitches into the spaces between stitches, fastening off, joining new colors, and working a chain stitch border. It's also a great opportunity to experiment with color combinations.

MATERIALS

Cascade Ultra Pima Fine (100% pima cotton; 1.75 oz/50 g; 136.5 yds /125 m)

Teal 3734 (yarn A)
Deep Coral 3767 (yarn B)
Cool Mint 3775 (yarn C)
Sand 3717 (yarn D)
Yellow Rose 3743 (yarn E)
Buff 3719 (yarn F)

HOOK SIZE

G-6 (4 mm) crochet hook

SKILL LEVEL

Beginner

GAUGE

Rounds 1–2 measure 2 in. (5 cm), so follow pattern, and at end of Round 2, you should have a measurement of 2 in. (5 cm).

FINISHED SIZE

6.5 in. (16.5 cm) in diameter

INSTRUCTIONS

Using yarn A, make a magic ring.

ROUND 1 Ch1, make 8sc into the ring and join with a sl st to the first sc.

ROUND 2 Ch4 (counts as 1dc, ch1), make 1dc in the same st, ch1, * (1dc, ch1, 1dc, ch1) into the next st; repeat from * 6 more times. Join with a sl st to 3rd ch of the beg ch4. Fasten off.

ROUND 3 Join yarn B in any ch-1 sp. Ch3, make 1dc in the same space (counts as dc2tog), ch2, * dc2tog, ch2 in the next ch-1 sp; repeat from * around. Join with a sl st to the top of the first cluster. Fasten off.

ROUND 4 Join yarn C to any ch-2 sp. Ch3, make 1dc in the same space (counts as dc2tog), ch2, * (dc2tog, ch2, dc2tog) in the next ch-2 sp, ch2, dc2tog in the next ch-2 sp, ch2; repeat from * to last ch-2 sp, (dc2tog, ch2, dc2tog) in the last ch-2 sp, ch2. Join with a sl st to the top of the first cluster. Fasten off.

ROUND 5 Join yarn D to any ch-2 sp to the right of a 2 cluster group. Ch3, make 1dc in the same space (counts as dc2tog), ch2, * (dc2tog, ch2, dc2tog) in the next ch-2 sp, (ch2, dc2tog in the next ch-2 sp) twice, ch2; repeat from * to the last 2 ch-2 sp, (dc2tog, ch2, dc2tog) in the next ch-2 sp, ch2, dc2tog in the last ch-2 sp, ch2. Join with a sl st to the top of the first cluster. Fasten off.

ROUND 6 Join yarn E to any ch-2 sp. Ch3, make 1dc in the same space (counts as dc2tog), ch2, * dc2tog, ch2 in the next ch-2 sp; repeat from * around. Join with a sl st to the top of the first cluster. Fasten off.

ROUND 7 Join yarn F to any ch-2 sp. Ch1, make 3sc in the same space, make 3sc in each ch-2 sp around. Join with a sl st to the first sc. Fasten off.

ROUND 8 Join yarn B to any sc to the right of a cluster from round 7. * ch4, skip 2 sts, sl st in the next st; repeat from * around. Join in the first ch of the beg ch4. Fasten off and weave in the ends.

Granny Hexagon

Give the Granny Square (see page 34) a new twist by creating a hexagon. Create the six corners by working additional double crochet stitches at six points around a central circle. The result is a geometric shape, which is ideal for making patchwork-style afghans and throws.

MATERIALS

Cascade Ultra Pima Fine
(100% pima cotton; 1.75 oz/50 g;
136.5 yds / 125 m)

Chocolate 3716 (yarn A)
Spring Green 3762 (yarn B)
Coral 3752 (yarn C)
Mint 3742 (yarn D)
Wood Violet 3709 (yarn E)

HOOK SIZE

G-6 (4 mm) crochet hook

SKILL LEVEL

Beginner

GAUGE

Rounds 1–2 measure 2.5 in.
(6 cm), so follow pattern, and at
end of Round 2, you should have a
measurement of 2.5 in. (6 cm).

FINISHED SIZE

4.25 in. (10.75 cm) in diameter

INSTRUCTIONS

Using yarn A, ch4; join into a ring.

ROUND 1 Ch4 (counts as 1dc, ch1),
* (1dc, ch1) into the ring; repeat from * 10
more times. Join with sl st to the 3rd ch of the
beg ch-4 sp. Fasten off.

ROUND 2 Using yarn B, join in any ch-1 sp, ch3
(counts as 1dc), make 1dc in the same space,
ch1, * 2dc in the next ch-1 sp, ch1; repeat from
* 10 more times. Join with sl st to the beg ch-3
sp. Fasten off.

ROUND 3 Using yarn C, join in any ch-1 sp.
Ch3 (counts as 1dc), make 2dc in the same
space, ch1, * 3dc in the next ch-1 sp, ch1;
repeat from * 10 more times. Join with a sl st to
the beg ch-3 sp. Fasten off.

ROUND 4 Using yarn D, join in any ch-1 sp.
Ch3 (counts as 1dc), make 2dc in the same
space, ch1, 3dc in the same space, make 3dc in
the next ch-1 sp, * (3dc, ch1, 3dc) in the next
ch-1 sp, make 3dc in the next ch-1 sp ; repeat
from * 4 more times. Join with a sl st to the beg
ch-3 sp. Fasten off.

ROUND 5 Using yarn E, join in any ch-1 sp.
Ch1, make 1sc in the same space, make 1sc in
each of the next 9 sts, * 2sc in the ch-1 sp, make
1sc in each of the next 9 sts; repeat from * 4
more times. Join with an invisible join to the first
sc made. Fasten off and weave in the ends.

TRY THIS...

A splash of teal brings an exciting
color contrast when used with a
selection of yellow and orange shades:

Sand 3717 (yarn A)

Teal 3734 (yarn B)

Tangerine 3750 (yarn C)

Sunshine 3764 (yarn D)

Paprika 3771 (yarn E)

Simple Sunburst

Double crochet stitches radiate from the center of this circular motif like the sun's rays. The circles are finished with a round of single crochet, which creates a neat border. Use one, two, or three colors to create bright color contrasts or soothing toning combinations.

MATERIALS

Cascade Ultra Pima Fine (100% pima cotton; 1.75 oz/50 g; 136.5 yds / 125 m)

Magenta 3703 (yarn A)
Deep Coral 3767 (yarn B)
Jade 3735 (yarn C)

HOOK SIZE

G-6 (4 mm) crochet hook

SKILL LEVEL

Beginner

GAUGE

Rounds 1–2 measure 2 in. (5 cm), so follow pattern, and at end of Round 2, you should have a measurement of 2 in. (5 cm).

FINISHED SIZE

3.5 in. (9 cm) in diameter

INSTRUCTIONS

Using yarn A, ch4 and join with sl st into a ring.

ROUND 1 Ch1, make 12sc into the ring; join with a sl st to the first sc.

ROUND 2 Ch5 (counts as 1dc, ch2), * 1dc into the next st, ch2; repeat from * 10 more times. Join with a sl st to the 3rd ch of the beg ch5. Fasten off.

ROUND 3 Using yarn B, join in any ch-2 sp. Ch3, make a dc2tog (counts as dc3tog) in the same space, ch4, * dc3tog in the next ch-2 sp, ch4; repeat from * 10 more times. Join with a sl st to the top of the first cluster. Fasten off.

ROUND 4 Using yarn C, join in the top of any cluster. Ch1, make 1sc in the same st, make 4sc in the next ch-4 sp, * 1sc in the top of the next cluster, make 4sc in the next ch-4 sp; repeat from * 10 more times. Join with an invisible join to the first sc. Fasten off.

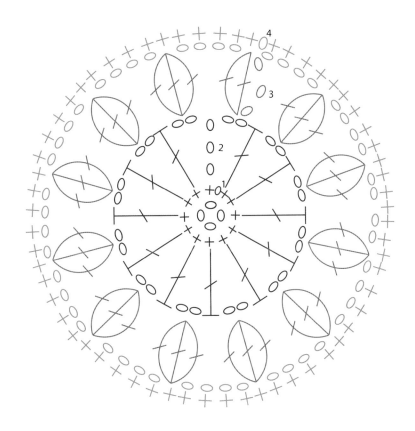

TRY THIS...

Make a simple motif by working the motif in a single color and using a complementary color for the border:

Wood Violet 3709 (yarn A and B)
Mint 3742 (yarn C)

Flower Mandala

In Tibetan Buddhism, mandalas are symbolic pictures of the universe and they are used during meditation. Every section of the mandala is significant and serves as a reminder of a guiding principle or an aspect of wisdom. Perhaps this is why making these colorful disks from crochet can be a therapeutic experience.

MATERIALS

Cascade Ultra Pima Fine
(100% pima cotton; 1.75 oz/50 g;
136.5 yds /125 m)

Deep Coral 3767 (yarn A)
Jade 3735 (yarn B)
Cool Mint 3775 (yarn C)
Chartreuse 3746 (yarn D)
Teal 3734 (yarn E)

HOOK SIZE

G-6 (4 mm) crochet hook

SKILL LEVEL

Beginner

GAUGE

Rounds 1–2 measure 2.75 in. (7 cm), so follow pattern, and at end of Round 2, you should have a measurement of 2.75 in. (7 cm).

FINISHED SIZE

6.5 in. (16.5 cm) in diameter

INSTRUCTIONS

Using yarn A, make a magic ring.

ROUND 1 Ch3 (counts as 1dc), make 11dc into the ring. Join with a sl st to the top of the beg ch-3 sp. Fasten off. (12dc)

PROJECT:

Embellished Basket

Take your crochet shopping or to the beach by attaching a mandala to a basket.

MATERIALS
1 mandala made using the Flower Mandala motif (see left). The sample shown uses Rico Creative Cotton Aran (100% cotton; 1.75 oz/50 g; 92 yds/84 m) Cherry 65 (yarn A), Natural 60 (yarn B), Sky Blue 37 (yarn C), Candy Pink 64 (yarn D), Petrol 47 (yarn E), or a similar worsted weight yarn, and a size H-8 (5mm) crochet hook

Straw basket measuring 10.5 x 13 x 7.5 in. (26.5 x 33 x 19 cm)

NOTIONS
Pins for blocking
Hot glue gun

GAUGE
Rounds 1–2 measure 4 in. (10 cm), so follow pattern, and at end of Round 2, you should have a measurement of 4 in. (10 cm).

FINISHED SIZE
Mandala measures 9 in. (23 cm) in diameter.

INSTRUCTIONS
Block the mandala by pinning it to shape and gently steaming it. Let dry.

Using a hot glue gun, attach the mandala to the front of a basket. Let set.

ROUND 2 Using yarn B, join in any st. Ch4, tr2tog (counts as tr3tog) in the same st, ch3, * tr3tog in the next st, ch3; repeat from * around. Join with a sl st to the top of the beg cluster. Fasten off. (12 tr3tog cls)

ROUND 3 With yarn C, join in any ch-3 sp. Ch3, make dc2tog (counts as dc3tog), ch2, dc3tog in the same space, ch2, * (dc3tog, ch2, dc3tog, ch2) in the next ch-3 sp; repeat from * around. Join with a sl st to the top of the beg cluster. Fasten off. (24 dc cls)

ROUND 4 With yarn D, join in any ch-2 sp. Ch3, make 1dc in same 2-ch sp (counts as dc2tog), ch3, * dc2tog, ch3, in the next ch-2 sp; repeat from * around. Join with a sl st to the top of beg ch-3 sp. Fasten off. (24 dc cls)

ROUND 5 With yarn A, join in any ch-3 sp. Ch3 (counts as 1dc), make 2dc in the same space, ch1; * 3dc in the next ch-3 sp, ch1; repeat from * around. Join with a sl st in the top of the beg ch-3 sp. Fasten off. (24 3dc groups)

ROUND 6 With yarn E, join in any ch-1 sp. Ch1, make 1sc in the same space, picot3 (ch3, sl st into 3rd ch from hook) ch3; * 1sc in the next ch-1 sp, picot3, ch3; repeat from * around. Join with a sl st to the first sc. Fasten off and weave in the ends.

Petal Mandala

Layers of stitches and color combine to make an appealing motif with a flower as the focus of a striped border. Dusky pastel shades are ideal for this motif, but it would work just as well—and provide a burst of color—if made in a selection of bright yarns.

MATERIALS

Cascade Ultra Pima Fine (100% pima cotton; 1.75 oz/50 g; 136.5 yds /125 m)

Yellow Rose 3743 (yarn A)
Sand 3717 (yarn B)
Ice 3736 (yarn C)
Buff 3719 (yarn D)
Deep Coral 3767 (yarn E)
Dark Sea Foam 3797 (yarn F)

HOOK SIZE

G-6 (4 mm) crochet hook

SKILL LEVEL

Intermediate

GAUGE

Rounds 1–3 measure 2.5 in. (6 cm), so follow pattern, and at end of Round 3, you should have a measurement of 2.5 in. (6 cm).

FINISHED SIZE

4.5 in. (11.5 cm) in diameter

INSTRUCTIONS

With yarn A, ch5; join with a sl st into a ring.

ROUND 1 Ch1, make 12sc into the ring and join with a sl st to the first sc. Fasten off. (12sc)

ROUND 2 With yarn B, join in any sc from previous round. Ch3 (counts as 1hdc, ch1), * 1hdc, ch1 into the next st; repeat from * around. Join with a sl st to the 2nd ch of the beg ch3. Fasten off. (12 hdc, 12 ch-1 sps)

ROUND 3 With yarn C, join in any ch-1 sp. Ch3, dc2tog in the same space (counts as dc3tog), ch2, * dc3tog in the next ch-1 sp, ch2; repeat from * around. Join with a sl st to the top of the beg cluster. Fasten off. (12 clusters)

ROUND 4 With yarn D, join in any ch-2 sp. Ch3 (counts as 1dc), make 3dc in the same space, * 4dc in the next ch-2 sp; repeat from * around. Join with a sl st to the top of the beg ch3. Fasten off. (12 4dc groups)

ROUND 5 With yarn E, join in the space between any 4dc. Ch1, make 1sc in the same space, ch2, skip 2 sts, * 1sc in the next space (between dc), ch2, skip 2 sts; repeat from * around (making each sc in the space between 2dc sts). Join with a sl st to the first sc. Fasten off. (24sc, 24 ch-2 sps)

ROUND 6 With yarn F, join in any ch-2 sp. Ch1, make 1sc in the same space, (1dc, ch1, 1dc, ch1, 1dc) in the next ch-2 sp, * 1sc in the next ch-2 sp, (1dc, ch1, 1dc, ch1, 1dc) in the next ch-2 sp; repeat from * around. Join with a sl st to the first sc. Fasten off and weave in the ends.

Lace Circle

A central disk surrounded by eight triangular sections forms a design, which is ideal to use as a table mat or doily. We have shown this motif worked in three colors, but the geometric pattern looks just as effective made in a single shade or from a variegated yarn.

MATERIALS

Cascade Ultra Pima Fine
(100% pima cotton; 1.75 oz/50 g;
136.5 yds /125 m)

Dark Sea Foam 3797 (yarn A)
Sage 3720 (yarn B)
Coral 3752 (yarn C)

HOOK SIZE

G-6 (4 mm) crochet hook

SKILL LEVEL

Intermediate

GAUGE

Rounds 1–2 measure 2.5 in.
(6 cm), so follow pattern, and at
end of Round 2, you should have a
measurement of 2.5 in. (6 cm).

FINISHED SIZE

7.25 in. (18.5 cm) in diameter

INSTRUCTIONS

Using yarn A, ch4 and join into a ring.

ROUND 1 Ch3, make 1dc into the ring (counts as dc2tog), ch2, * dc2tog, ch2, repeat from * 6 more times. Join with a sl st to the top of the beg cluster. Fasten off. (8 clusters)

ROUND 2 Using yarn B, join in any ch-2 sp. Ch3 (counts as 1dc), make 2dc in the same space, ch2, * 3dc in next ch-2 sp, ch2; repeat from * around 6 more times. Join with a sl st to the top of the beg ch3.

ROUND 3 Ch3 (counts as 1dc), make 1dc in the same st, make 1dc in next st, make 2dc in the next st, ch2, miss 2 ch, * 2dc in the next st, make 1dc in the next st, make 2dc in the next st, ch2, miss 2 ch; repeat from * around 6 more times. Join with a sl st to the top of the beg ch3.

ROUND 4 Ch3 (counts as 1dc), make 1dc in the same st, make 1dc in the next 3 sts, make 2dc in the next st, ch2, miss 2 ch, * 2dc in the next st, make 1dc in the next 3 sts, make 2dc in the next st, ch2, miss 2 ch; repeat from * around 6 more times. Join with a sl st to the top of the beg ch3.

ROUND 5 Ch3 (counts as 1dc), make 1dc in the same st, make 1dc in the next 5 sts,

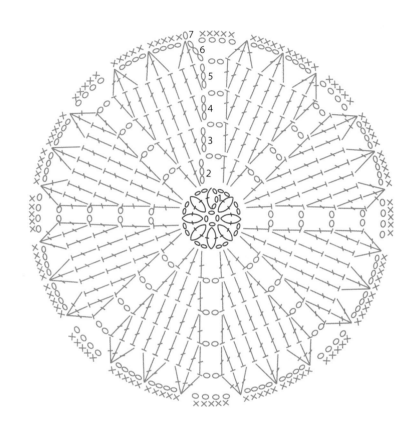

make 2dc in the next st, ch2, miss 2 ch, * 2dc in the next st, make 1dc in the next 5 sts, make 2dc in the next st, ch2, miss 2 ch; repeat from * around 6 more times. Join with a sl st to the top of the beg ch3.

ROUND 6 Ch3, dc2tog over the next 2 sts (counts as dc3tog), ch4, (dc3tog over the next 3 sts, ch4) twice, miss 2 ch, * (dc3tog over the next 3 sts, ch4) 3 times, miss 2

ch; repeat from * around 6 more times. Join with a sl st to the beg cluster. Fasten off.

ROUND 7 Using yarn C, join in any ch-4 space. Ch1, make 5sc in the same sp, * 5sc in the next ch-4 sp; repeat from * around. Join with a sl st to the first sc. Fasten off and weave in the ends.

Dainty Mandala

The points of a picot edge add to the airy feel of this Dainty Mandala, made from rounds of chain stitch and double crochet V-stitches. Select bright colors to create a series of strong contrasts in this design, or select ombre shades to create a subtle finish.

MATERIALS

Cascade Ultra Pima Fine
(100% pima cotton; 1.75 oz/50 g;
136.5 yds /125 m)

Natural 3718 (yarn A)
Primrose 3712 (yarn B)
Teal 3734 (yarn C)
Cool Mint 3775 (yarn D)
Pansy 3779 (yarn E)

HOOK SIZE

G-6 (4 mm) crochet hook

SKILL LEVEL

Intermediate

GAUGE

Rounds 1–2 measure 2.5 in.
(6 cm), so follow pattern, and at
end of Round 2, you should have a
measurement of 2.5 in. (6 cm).

FINISHED SIZE

5 in. (12.5 cm) in diameter

SPECIAL STITCHES

V-stitch (V-st) see page 139

INSTRUCTIONS

Using yarn A, ch4 and join in a ring.

ROUND 1 Ch3 (counts as 1dc), make 15dc in the ring. Join with a sl st to the 3rd ch of the beg ch3. Fasten off. (16 dc)

ROUND 2 Using yarn B, join in any st. Ch4 (counts as 1dc, ch1), * 1dc, ch1 in the next st; repeat from * around. Join with a sl st to 3rd ch of the beg ch4. Fasten off. (16 dc, 16 ch-1 sps)

ROUND 3 Using yarn C, join in any ch-1 sp. Ch3 (counts as 1dc), make 1dc, ch1 in the same sp, * 2dc, ch1 in the next ch-1 sp; repeat from * around. Join with a sl st to 3rd ch of the beg ch4. Fasten off. (32 dc, 16 ch-1 sps)

ROUND 4 Using yarn D, join in any ch-1 sp. Ch4, make 1dc in same sp (counts as -V-st), ch1, * V-st, ch1 in the next ch-1 sp; repeat from * around. Join with a sl st to the 3rd ch of the beg ch4. (16 V-st, 16 ch-1 sps)

ROUND 5 Using yarn E, join in ch-1 of any V-st. Ch1, make 1sc in the same space, ch2, ch3, sl st into 3rd ch from hook (picot made), ch2, * 1sc into next V-st, ch2, picot3, ch2; repeat from * around. Join with a sl st to the first sc. Fasten off and weave in the ends. (16 picots)

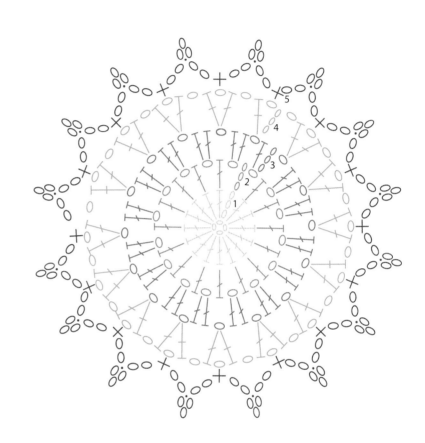

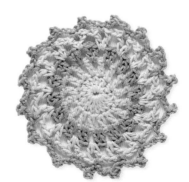

TRY THIS...
Combine cool ice-cream shades to create a vintage-style color palette:

Mint 3742 (yarn A)
Yellow Rose 3743 (yarn B)
Sand 3717 (yarn C)
Ice 3736 (yarn D)
Coral 3752 (yarn E)

MATERIALS

Scraps of Scheepjeswol Cotton 8 yarn (100% cotton;1.75 oz/ 50 g;186 yds/170 m), or a similar 4-ply yarn, in 11 colors (A–K)

NOTIONS

C-2 (3 mm) crochet hook; adjust size if necessary to obtain correct gauge

Tapestry needle

Pins for blocking

GAUGE

Rounds 1–2 measure 2 in. (5 cm), so follow pattern, and at end of Round 2, you should have a measurement of 2 in. (5 cm).

FINISHED SIZE

11 in. (28 cm) diameter

SPECIAL STITCHES

V-stitch (V-st) see page 139

Picot ch5, sl st into first ch

Lace Mandala

The calming rhythm of crocheting a mandala design is enhanced when each round is worked in a contrasting brightly colored yarn. This Lace Mandala is made using the first four rounds of the Dainty Mandala (see page 20) at its center. The motif is then extended by adding seven more rounds. The result is as a light, open circle using a 4-ply yarn.

INSTRUCTIONS

Using yarns A–D, work Rounds 1–4 of the Dainty Mandala motif (see page 20).

ROUND 5 Using yarn E, join in any ch-1 sp in any V-st. Ch4, make 1dc in same sp (counts as first V-st), ch3. * V-st, ch3 in the next ch-1 sp; repeat from * around. Join with a sl st to the 3rd ch of the beg ch4. Fasten off. (16 V-st, 16 ch-3 sps)

ROUND 6 Using yarn F, join in any ch-1 sp. Ch4, make 1dc in same sp (counts as first V-st), ch4. * V-st, ch4 in the next ch-1 sp; repeat from * around. Join with a sl st to the 3rd ch of the beg ch4. Fasten off. (16 V-st, 16 ch-4 sps)

ROUND 7 Using yarn G, join in any ch-1 sp. Ch4, make 1dc in same sp (counts as first V-st), ch1. V-st, ch1 in the next ch-4 sp, * V-st, ch1 in the next ch-1 sp, V-st, ch1 in the next ch-4 sp; repeat from * around. Join with a sl st to the 3rd ch of the beg ch4. Fasten off. (32 V-st, 32 ch-1 sps)

ROUND 8 Using yarn H, join in any V-st ch-1 sp. Ch4, make 1dc in same sp (counts as first V-st), ch2. * V-st, ch2 in the next ch-1 (V-st) sp; repeat from * around. Join with a sl st to the 3rd ch of the beg ch4. Fasten off. (32 V-st, 32 ch-2 sps)

ROUND 9 Using yarn I, repeat Round 8 (32 V-st, 32 ch-2 sps)

ROUND 10 Using yarn J, join in any ch-1 sp in any V-st. Ch1, make 1sc in the same st, ch1, [3dc, ch2, 3dc] in the next ch-1 sp, ch1, * 1sc in the next ch-1 sp, ch1, [3dc, ch2, 3dc] in the next ch-1 sp, ch1; repeat from * around. Join with a sl st to the first sc. Fasten off.

ROUND 11 Using yarn K, join yarn to the top of first dc made in Round 10. Ch3, make 1dc in the next 2 sts, (dc2, picot st, dc2) in the ch-2 sp, make 1dc in the next 3 sts, ch1, * 1dc in the next 3dc, (dc2, picot st, dc2) in the ch-2 sp, make 1dc in the next 3dc; repeat from * around. Join with a sl st to the top of the beg ch3. Fasten off.

FINISHING
Weave in all the ends with your tapestry needle. Block your mandala by pinning it into shape and gently steam it using your iron.

Lace Flower

A simple chain-stitch lace border surrounds the double-crochet petals of this flower motif. They look fresh and modern when worked in bright colors, but you can create a classic lace look by using neutrals like white and pastels.

MATERIALS

Cascade Ultra Pima Fine
(100% pima cotton; 1.75 oz/50 g; 136.5 yds /125 m)

Aqua 3732 (yarn A)
Wood Violet 3709 (yarn B)
Ice 3736 (yarn C)

HOOK SIZE

G-6 (4 mm) crochet hook

SKILL LEVEL

Intermediate

GAUGE

Rounds 1–2 measure 2.75 in. (7 cm), so follow pattern, and at end of Round 2, you should have a measurement of 2.75 in. (7 cm).

FINISHED SIZE

3.75 in. (9.5 cm) in diameter

INSTRUCTIONS

Using yarn A, make a magic ring.

ROUND 1 Ch4 (counts as 1dc, ch1), * make 1dc, ch1 into the ring; repeat from * 6 more times. Join with a sl st to the 3rd ch of the beg ch4. Fasten off. (8 dc, 8 ch-1 sps)

ROUND 2 Using yarn B, join in the top of any dc. Ch1, make 1sc in the same st, * ch3, tr3tog in the next ch-1 sp, ch3, make 1sc in the next dc; repeat from * 7 more times, ending the last st with a sl st in the first sc. Fasten off. (8 tr3tog clusters)

ROUND 3 Using yarn C, join in any sc from Round 2. Ch5 (counts as 1dc, ch2), make 1sc in the top of the next tr3tog cl, * ch2, make 1dc in the next sc, ch2, make 1sc in the next tr3tog cl; repeat from * 6 more times. Ch1, join with 1hdc in the 3rd ch of the beg ch5 (counts as the last ch-2 sp). Do not fasten off.

ROUND 4 Ch1, make 1sc under the hdc just made. Ch4,* 1sc in the next ch-2 sp, ch4; repeat from * around. Join with a sl st in the first sc. Fasten off.

TRY THESE...

Bright orange and yellow outlined with pale purple create a burst of summer color:

Tangerine 3750 (yarn A)
Buttercup 3748 (yarn B)
Wood Violet 3709 (yarn C)

MATERIALS

Cascade Ultra Pima Fine (100% pima cotton; 1.75 oz/50 g; 136.5 yds /125 m), or a similar sportweight yarn

True Black 3754 (MC) x 2 balls
Tangerine 3750 x 1 ball
Buttercup 3748 x 1 ball
Paprika 3771 x 1 ball
Natural 3718 x 1 ball
Sand 3717 x 1 ball
Spring Crocus 3815 x 1 ball
Grapeade 3816 x 1 ball
Coral 3752 x 1 ball
Deep Coral 3767 x 1 ball

NOTIONS

G-6 (4 mm) crochet hook; adjust size if necessary to obtain correct gauge

Tapestry needle

GAUGE

Rounds 1–2 measure 2.75 in. (7 cm), so follow pattern, and at end of Round 2, you should have a measurement of 2.75 in. (7 cm).

FINISHED SIZE

18 in x 52 in. (46 x 132 cm)

NOTES

After completing the first motif, the remaining motifs are joined in all the ch-3 sps while making Round 5, and in the ch-5 sps from Round 5.

PROJECT

Lace Flower Shawl

Once you've chosen the colors for this shawl there's no need to think about how to combine them—simply pick a yarn at random, start to stitch, and relax. The motifs are joined together as you crochet the final round of each circle, so make sure you are happy with the way you have arranged them before you start to assemble the shawl. The result is a swathe of flowers that will keep you warm on a summer evening.

INSTRUCTIONS

Make a total of 48 motifs by working Rounds 1-4 of the Lace Flower motif (see page 24) using different color combinations. Weave in the ends with your yarn needle.

Lay out your motifs on a table in a pleasing combination.

FIRST MOTIF

ROUND 5 Using the MC, join in any ch-4 sp. Ch1 and make 1sc in the same space, (ch3, 1sc in the next ch-4 sp) twice, * ch3, (dc2tog, ch5, dc2tog) in the next ch-4 sp, (ch3, 1sc in the next ch-4 sp) 3 times; repeat from * twice more, ch3, (dc2tog, ch5, dc2tog) in the next ch-4 sp, ch3. Join with a sl st to the first sc made. Fasten off.

SUBSEQUENT MOTIFS

With the right sides facing and starting at the top right corner of your shawl, join the 2nd motif as follows:

ROUND 5 (joining round) Using the MC, join in any ch-4 sp. Ch1 and make 1sc in the same space, (ch3, 1sc in next ch-4 sp) twice, ch3, (dc2tog, ch2, sl st in the corresponding corner ch-5 sp in the first motif, ch2, dc2tog) in the next ch-4 sp, (ch1, sl st in the corresponding ch-3 sp in the first motif, ch1, 1sc in the next ch-4 sp) 3 times, ch1, sl st in corresponding ch-3 sp in first motif, ch1, (dc2tog, ch2, sl st in the corresponding corner ch-5 sp in the first motif, ch2, dc2tog) in the next ch-4 sp, * (ch3, 1sc in the next ch-4 sp) 3 times, ch3, (dc2tog, ch5, dc2tog) in the next ch-4 sp; repeat from * once more, ch3. Join with a sl st to the first sc made. Fasten off.

Continue to join each motif to the previous one like this until you have a strip of four motifs.

You will continue joining each row in the same way until you have 12 rows of 4 motifs. When joining to 2 motifs, sl st into the corner of the motif directly above. When joining to 3 motifs, sl st into the center where 3 motifs meet. Weave in the ends with a yarn needle.

BORDER

Join the MC in any ch-3 sp. Ch1 and make * 1sc in the same space, ch3, make 1dc in the sc just made, make 1sc in the next ch-3 sp; repeat from * around all four sides; work (1sc in the same space, ch3, 1dc in the sc just made) twice, in the corner ch-5 sps, Join with a sl st to the first sc made. Fasten off.

Block the shawl into shape by steaming.

Flower Hexagon

Layers of stitches and color combine to make an appealing motif with a flower as the focus. Here a pop of pink contrasts with a border of pale blue and beige, but primary colors would work well to create a funky modern finish.

MATERIALS

Cascade Ultra Pima Fine
(100% pima cotton; 1.75 oz/50 g;
136.5 yds / 125 m)

Chartreuse 3746 (yarn A)
Sand 3717 (yarn B)
Deep Coral 3767 (yarn C)
Ice 3736 (yarn D)

HOOK SIZE

G-6 (4 mm) crochet hook

SKILL LEVEL

Advanced

GAUGE

Rounds 1–3 measure 2.75 in.
(7 cm), so follow pattern, and at
end of Round 3, you should have
a measurement of 2.75 in.
(7 cm).

FINISHED SIZE

5 in. (12.5 cm) in diameter

INSTRUCTIONS
Using yarn A, make a magic ring.

ROUND 1 Ch2 (counts as 1hdc), make 11hdc into the ring, sl st to the beg ch2 to join. Fasten off. (12 hdc)

ROUND 2 Using yarn B, join in the space between 2hdc. Ch3, make 1dc (counts as dc2tog) in the same space, ch1, *dc2tog in the next space, ch1; repeat from * around. Join with a sl st to the first cluster. Fasten off.

ROUND 3 Using yarn C, join with a sl st in any ch-1 sp. Make 7dc in the next ch-1 sp, * sl st in the next ch-1 sp, make 7dc in the next ch-1 sp ; repeat from * around. Join with a sl st to the first dc. Fasten off.

ROUND 4 Using yarn D, join by inserting the hook under a sl st from round 3. Ch7 (counts as 1tr, ch3), skip the next 3 sts, * sl st in the next st, (center st of 7dc), skip the next 3 sts, ch3, make 1tr under the next sl st, skip the next 3 sts, ch3; repeat from * around to the end, sl st in the next st, miss the next 3 sts, ch3. Join with a sl st to the 4th ch of the beg ch7. Do not fasten off.

ROUND 5 Sl st into the next ch-3 sp. Ch3 (counts as 1dc), make 3dc in the same space, make 4dc in the next ch-3 sp, ch2, * (4dc in the next ch-3 sp) twice, ch2; repeat from * 4 more times. Join with a sl st to the top of the beg ch-3 sp. Fasten off.

ROUND 6 Using yarn B, join in any ch-2 sp. Ch5 (counts as 1dc, ch2), make 1dc in the same space, make 1dc in each of the next 8 sts, * (1dc, ch2, 1dc) in the next ch-2 sp, make 1dc in each of the next 8 sts; repeat from * 4 more times. Join with a sl st to 3rd ch of the beg ch5. Fasten off and weave in the ends.

Pinwheel

The abstract sections of this Pinwheel design form striped sails, which rotate around a central six-petaled flower. The picot stitches around the edge of the circle may look complicated but they are simply lengths of chain stitches secured with slip stitches.

MATERIALS

Cascade Ultra Pima Fine
(100% pima cotton; 1.75 oz/50 g;
136.5 yds /125 m)

Lipstick Red 3755 (yarn A)
Deep Coral 3767 (yarn B)
Coral 3752 (yarn C)
Buttercup 3748 (yarn D)

HOOK SIZE

G-6 (4 mm) crochet hook

SKILL LEVEL

Advanced

GAUGE

Rounds 1–3 measure 2.5 in.
(6 cm), so follow pattern, and at end of Round 3, you should have a measurement of 2.5 in. (6 cm).

FINISHED SIZE

6.25 in. (16 cm) in diameter at widest point

INSTRUCTIONS

Using yarn A, make a magic ring.

ROUND 1 Ch1, make 6sc into the ring. Join with a sl st to the first sc.

ROUND 2 Ch3 (counts as 1dc), make 1dc in the first sc, ch2, * 2dc, ch2 in the next sc; repeat from * 4 more times. Join with a sl st to the top of the beg ch3. Fasten off.

ROUND 3 Using yarn B, join in any ch-2 sp. Ch3 (counts as 1dc), make 3dc in the same space, ch2, * 4dc in the next ch-2 sp, ch2; repeat from * 4 more times. Join with a sl st to the top of the beg ch3. Fasten off.

ROUND 4 Using yarn C, join in yarn at top of beg ch3 from previous round. Ch3 (counts as 1dc), make 1dc in each of the next 2 sts, make 3dc in the next st, ch3, * 1dc in the next 3 sts, make 3dc in the next st, ch3; repeat from * 4 more times. Join with a sl st to the top of the beg ch3. Fasten off.

ROUND 5 Using yarn D, join with a sl st at top of beg ch3 from previous round. Ch3 (counts as 1dc), make 1dc in each of the next 4 sts, make 3dc in the next st, ch3, * 1dc in the next 5 sts, make 3dc in the next st, ch3; repeat from * 4 more times. Join with a sl st to the top of the beg ch3. Fasten off.

ROUND 6 Using yarn A, join with a sl st at top of beg ch3 from previous round. Ch2, make 1dc in each of the next 6 sts, make 3dc in the next st, ch3, sl st in the first ch from the hook (picot made), (ch3, sl st in the 3rd ch from the hook) 2 more times, ch3, sl st into the top of the next dc, * ch2, make 1dc in each of the next 6 sts, make

3dc in the next st, (ch3, sl st in the 3rd ch from the hook) 3 times, ch3, sl st into the top of the next dc; repeat from * 4 more times. Join with a sl st into the base of the beg ch2. Fasten off and weave in the ends.

Squares

A series of crochet squares can be used to create soothing blocks of color thanks to the combinations of shades used. Join two squares together to make a simple pincushion, or experiment with multiple squares to create a pillow cover or blanket.

PINCUSHION
Every sewing basket needs a pincushion, and who could resist this colorful example? Whether you're an expert dressmaker, or restrict your sewing to essential repairs, use one of these to keep your pins in order. For the instructions to make this design, see page 46.

Granny Square

It's no wonder that the Granny Square is a classic crochet motif and one of the first many people learn to make—its simple combination of chains and groups of double crochet stitches are quick to work and easy to remember. Work it in one color, switch colors every round, or alternate every two rounds for different visual effects.

MATERIALS

Cascade Ultra Pima Fine
(100% pima cotton; 1.75 oz/50 g;
136.5 yds / 125 m)

Coral 3752 (yarn A)
Cool Mint 3775 (yarn B)
Deep Coral 3767 (yarn C)
Natural 3718 (yarn D)
Ice 3736 (yarn E)

HOOK SIZE

G-6 (4 mm) crochet hook

SKILL LEVEL

Beginner

GAUGE

Rounds 1–2 measure 2 in.
(5 cm), so follow pattern, and at
end of Round 2, you should have a
measurement of 2 in. (5 cm).

FINISHED SIZE

4.5 in. (11.5 cm) square

TRY THIS...

Use bright colors to create a bold motif by changing color every 2 rounds:

Chartreuse 3746 (yarn A)
Deep Coral 3767 (yarns B and C)
Cool Mint 3775 (yarns D and E)

INSTRUCTIONS

Using yarn A, ch4 and join with a sl st into a ring.

ROUND 1 Ch3 (counts as first dc), 2dc into ring, ch2, * 3dc into ring, ch2; repeat from * 2 more times, join with sl st to the top of beg ch3. Fasten off.

ROUND 2 Join yarn B to any ch-2 space, ch3 (counts as first dc), (2dc, ch2, 3dc) into same space (corner), * ch1, (3dc, ch2, 3dc) into next ch-2 space; repeat from * 2 more times, ch1, join with sl st to the top of beg ch3. Fasten off.

ROUND 3 Join yarn C to any ch-2 space, ch3 (counts as first dc), (2dc, ch2, 3dc) into same space, * ch1, 3dc in next ch-1 space, ch1, ** (3dc, ch2, 3dc) into next ch-2 space; repeat from * 2 more times, and from * to ** once, join with sl st to the top of beg ch3. Fasten off.

ROUND 4 Join yarn D to any ch-2 space, ch3 (counts as first dc), (2dc, ch2, 3dc) into same space, * (ch1, 3dc) in each ch-1 space on side of square, ch1, ** (3dc, ch2, 3dc) into next ch-2 sp; repeat from * 2 more times, and from * to ** once, join with sl st to the top of beg ch3. Fasten off.

ROUND 5 Join yarn E to any ch-2 space, ch3 (counts as first dc), (2dc, ch2, 3dc) into same space, * (ch1, 3dc) in each ch-1 sp on side of square, ch1, ** (3dc, ch2, 3dc) into next ch-2 sp; repeat from * 2 more times, and from * to ** once, join with sl st to the top of beg ch3. Fasten off.

Bull's-eye Square

A combination of half double crochet and double crochet stitches are used to transform the circular center of this motif into a square block. The result has a solid construction and suits both contrasting and complementary color schemes.

MATERIALS

Cascade Ultra Pima Fine (100% pima cotton; 1.75 oz/50 g; 136.5 yds /125 m)

Coral 3752 (yarn A)
Sand 3717 (yarn B)
Deep Coral 3767 (yarn C)

HOOK SIZE

G-6 (4 mm) crochet hook

SKILL LEVEL

Intermediate

GAUGE

Rounds 1–2 measure 2 in. (5 cm), so follow pattern, and at end of Round 2, you should have a measurement of 2 in. (5 cm).

FINISHED SIZE

4.25 in. (10.75 cm) square

INSTRUCTIONS

Using yarn A, make a magic ring.

ROUND 1 Ch3 (counts as first dc), 11dc into magic ring; join with a sl st to top of the beg ch3. (12 dc)

ROUND 2 Ch3 (counts as first dc), 2dc in next st and each st around; end with 1dc in bottom of starting ch3. Join with a sl st to the top of the beg ch3. Fasten off. (24dc)

ROUND 3 Using yarn B, join in any st from the previous round. Ch3 (counts as first dc), 4dc in same st (corner), 1hdc in next st, 1sc in next 3 sts, 1hdc in next st, * 5dc in next st, 1hdc in next st, 1sc in next 3 sts, 1hdc in next st; repeat from * 2 more times. Join with a sl st to the top of the beg ch3.

ROUND 4 Ch3 (counts as first dc), 1dc in next st, 5dc in next st (corner), 1dc in next 9 sts, (5dc in next st, 1dc in next 9 sts) 2 times, 5dc in next st, 1dc in next 7 sts. Join with a sl st to the top of the beg ch3. Fasten off.

ROUND 5 Using yarn C, join in any st from the previous round. Ch3 (counts as first dc), make 1dc in each st around. Make 5dc in each corner (in 3rd st of 5dc of previous round). Join with a sl st to the top of the beg ch3. Fasten off.

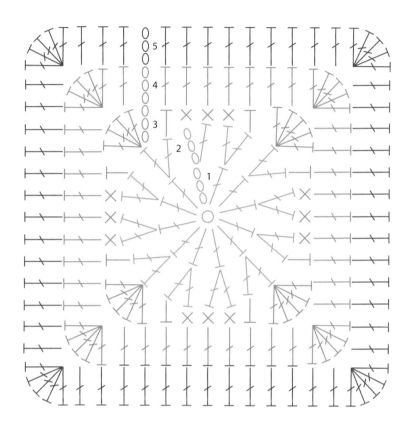

Cluster Square

Clusters of double crochet stitches create a star-shaped center and diagonal stripes within this square motif. The stripes are separated by rows of double crochet stitches. We combined ombre pinks with a bright turquoise for a pop of color, but neutrals work well here too.

MATERIALS

Cascade Ultra Pima Fine
(100% pima cotton; 1.75 oz/50 g;
136.5 yds /125 m)

Cool Mint 3775 (yarn A)
Coral 3752 (yarn B)
Deep Coral 3767 (yarn C)
Lipstick Red 3755 (yarn D)

HOOK SIZE

G-6 (4 mm) crochet hook

SKILL LEVEL

Intermediate

GAUGE

Rounds 1–2 measure 2.5 in.
(6 cm), so follow pattern, and at
end of Round 2, you should have a
measurement of 2.5 in. (6 cm).

FINISHED SIZE

5.5 in. (14 cm) square

INSTRUCTIONS

Using yarn A, ch5 and join with sl st into ring.

ROUND 1 Ch2 (counts as 1dc), dc2tog into ring, ch3, * dc3tog into ring, ch2, ** dc3tog into ring, ch3; repeat from * 2 more times, and from * to ** once more; join with sl st to the top of the beg ch2. Fasten off. (8 clusters)

ROUND 2 Using yarn B, join in any ch-3 sp, ch2 (counts as 1dc), (dc2tog, ch3, dc3tog) into same space, *ch2, 3dc into ch-2 sp, ch2, ** (dc3tog, ch3, dc3tog) into ch-3 sp; repeat from * 2 more times, and from * to ** once more; join with sl st to the top of the beg ch2. Fasten off.

ROUND 3 Using yarn C, join in any ch-3 sp, ch2 (counts as 1dc), (dc2tog, ch3, dc3tog) into same space, * ch2, 2dc in ch-2 sp, 1dc in next 3 sts, 2dc in ch-2 sp, ch2, ** (dc3tog, ch3, dc3tog) into ch-3 sp; repeat from * 2 more times, and from * to ** once more, join with sl st to the top of the beg ch2.

ROUND 4 Sl st into next ch-3 sp, ch2 (counts as 1dc), (dc2tog, ch3, dc3tog) into same space, * ch2, 2dc in ch-2 sp, 1dc in next 7 sts, 2dc in ch-2 sp, ch2, ** (dc3tog, ch3, dc3tog) into ch-3 sp; repeat from * 2 more times, and from * to

** once more; join with sl st to the top of the beg ch2. Fasten off.

ROUND 5 Using yarn D, join in any ch-3 sp, ch2 (counts as 1dc), (dc2tog, ch3, dc3tog) into same space, * ch2, 2dc in ch-2 sp, 1dc in next 11 sts, 2dc in ch-2 sp, ch2, ** (dc3tog, ch3, dc3tog) into ch-3 sp; repeat from * 2 more times, and from * to ** once more; join with sl st to the top of the beg ch2. Fasten off.

ROUND 6 Using yarn A, join to any st from round 5, ch1 (counts as first sc), sc into each st around, making 1sc on the top of each cluster. Make 2sc in each ch-2 sp, and (1sc, ch2, 1sc) in each corner ch-3 sp. Join with a sl st to first dc.

Mexican Tile Square

The cluster of double crochet stitches in the center of this motif contrasts with the airy borders of the same stitch that surround it. Starting the motif with a magic ring enables you to make the hole in the center as small as possible.

MATERIALS

Cascade Ultra Pima Fine
(100% pima cotton; 1.75 oz/50 g;
136.5 yds /125 m)

Lipstick Red 3755 (yarn A)
Deep Coral 3767 (yarn B)
Cool Mint 3775 (yarn C)
Buttercup 3748 (yarn D)
Buff 3719 (yarn E)

HOOK SIZE

G-6 (4 mm) crochet hook

SKILL LEVEL

Intermediate

GAUGE

Rounds 1–2 measure 2 in.
(5 cm), so follow pattern, and at
end of Round 2, you should have a
measurement of 2 in. (5 cm).

FINISHED SIZE

3.75 in. (9.5 cm) square

INSTRUCTIONS

With yarn A, make a magic ring.

ROUND 1 Ch3 (counts as first dc), make 15dc into the ring. Join with a sl st to the top of the beg ch3. Fasten off. (16dc)

ROUND 2 With yarn B, join to any st. Ch3 (counts as first dc), make 1dc in the next 2 sts, 2dc in the next st, ch4, *1dc in the next 3 sts, 2dc in the next st, and ch4. Repeat from * 2 more times. Join with a sl st to the top of the beg ch3. Fasten off.

ROUND 3 With yarn C, ch3 (counts as first dc). Make 1dc in the next 4 sts, [3dc, ch4, 3dc] in the corner ch-4 sp, * 1dc in the next 5 sts, [3dc, ch4, 3dc] in the corner ch-4 sp. Repeat from * 2 more times. Join with a sl st to the top of the beg ch3. Fasten off.

ROUND 4 With yarn D, ch1. Make 1sc in each st around, and work 4sc in each corner ch-4 sp. Join with a sl st to the first sc. Fasten off.

ROUND 5 Using yarn E, ch1. Make 1sc in each st around, and work 1 ch between the 2sc at the center of each corner. Sl st to join in the first sc. Fasten off.

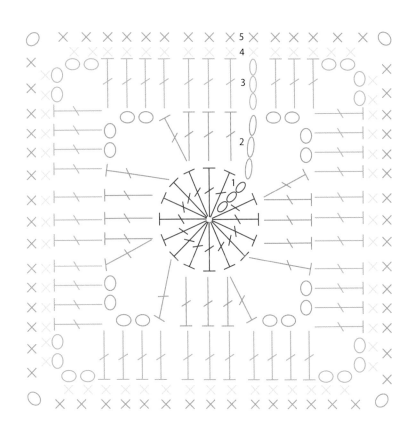

TRY THIS...

Don't be afraid to mix cool blues and purples with a shot of green:

Pansy 3779 (yarn A)
Chartreuse 3746 (yarn B)
Wood Violet 3709 (yarn C)
Cool Mint 3775 (yarn D)
Gray 3729 (yarn E)

MATERIALS

DK cotton yarn in a number of colors

3.5 oz (100 g) DK cotton yarn (MC)
1.75 oz (50 g) DK cotton yarn (CC1)
1.75 oz (50 g) DK cotton yarn (CC2)

NOTIONS

G-6 (4 mm) crochet hook; adjust hook size if necessary to obtain correct gauge

Tapestry needle

GAUGE

Rounds 1–2 measure 2.25 in. (5.7 cm), so follow pattern, and at end of Round 2, you should have a measurement of 2.25 in. (5.7 cm).

FINISHED SIZE

About 48 x 60 in. (122 x 152.5 cm)

PROJECT

Mexican Tiles Blanket

Walls covered in traditional handpainted Mexican tiles captivate with their gloriously bold and eclectic use of clashing, yet always sympathetic, colors and patterns. This relaxed, "anything-goes" approach takes the stress out of making a large project—simply focus on one square at a time, and use whatever yarn you have on hand. It also makes this blanket an excellent stash buster for all your yarn.

INSTRUCTIONS

Work 120 squares using the Mexican Tile motif (see page 40) in a combination of colors. Arrange the squares in a layout of your choice in twelve rows made up of ten squares across. Use MC to slip stitch the squares together: With the right sides of the squares to be joined facing, sl st in the outer loops only. Join each row horizontally using this method, and then join the squares vertically until the blanket is complete.

Weave in the ends.

BORDER

Use the MC for the first two rounds of the border, and use two CC colors for Rounds 3 and 4.

Using MC, and with the right side facing you, join with a sl st to any st on the outer edge.

ROUND 1 Ch1, sc evenly in each st around the border, working 2sc at the join where the squares meet. Make (1sc, ch2, 1sc) in each corner ch-1 sp. Join with a sl st to the first sc.

ROUND 2 Ch3 (counts as first dc), dc in each st around, and work (2dc, ch2, 2dc) in each corner ch-2 sp. Join with a sl st to the top of the beg ch3. Fasten off and change to CC1.

ROUND 3 Ch3 (counts as first dc), and dc in each st around. Work (2dc, ch1, 2dc) in each corner ch-2 sp. Join with a sl st to the top of the beg ch3. Fasten off and change to CC2.

ROUND 4 Ch1, and sc in each st around. Work 2sc in the corner ch-1 sp. Sl st to join in the first sc. Fasten off.

Weave in the ends.

Anemone Square

Working two or three double crochet stitches together to create clusters turns these simple stitches into the radiating petals of the flower in the center of this square. The resulting flowers are bordered by a frame of two rounds of double crochet stitches.

MATERIALS

Cascade Ultra Pima Fine (100% pima cotton; 1.75 oz/50 g; 136.5 yds /125 m)

Sand 3717 (yarn A)
Pansy 3779 (yarn B)
Cool Mint 3775 (yarn C)
Wood Violet 3709 (yarn D)

HOOK SIZE

G-6 (4 mm) crochet hook

SKILL LEVEL

Intermediate

GAUGE

Rounds 1–2 measure 2.5 in. (6 cm), so follow pattern, and at end of Round 2, you should have a measurement of 2.5 in. (6 cm).

FINISHED SIZE

4 in. (10 cm) square

INSTRUCTIONS

With yarn A, make a magic ring.

ROUND 1 Ch4 (counts as 1dc, ch1), (1dc, ch1) 11 times into the ring. Join with a sl st to the 3rd ch of the beg ch4. Fasten off. (12 dc, 12 ch-1 sps)

ROUND 2 Using yarn B, join in any ch-1 sp. Ch3, dc2tog in the same sp, ch3, *dc3tog in the next ch-1 sp, ch3; repeat from * in each ch-1 sp. Join with a sl st to the beg ch3. Fasten off. (12 clusters, 12 ch-3 sps)

ROUND 3 Using yarn C, join in any ch-3 sp. Ch1, 3sc in the same sp, (1hdc, 2dc) in the next ch-3 sp, (1dc, ch2, 1dc) on top of the next cluster (corner made), (2dc, 1hdc) in the next ch-3 sp, *3sc in the next sp, (1hdc, 2dc) in the next sp, (1dc, ch2, 1dc) on top of the next cluster, (2dc, 1hdc) in the next sp; repeat from * 2 more times. Join with a sl st to the first sc. Fasten off.

ROUND 4 Using yarn D, join in any st from the previous row. Ch2 (counts as first dc), make 1dc in each st around. Make (2dc, ch2, 2dc) in each ch-2 corner sp. Join with a sl st to the beg ch2. Fasten off.

TRY THIS...
Use summery yellow and green as a contrast to bright coral pinks:

Buttercup 3748 (yarn A)
Lipstick Red 3755 (yarn B)
Spring Green 3762 (yarn C)
Deep Coral 3767 (yarn D)

Retro Square

This graphic motif is enhanced by double crochet spike stitches—elongated double crochet stitches that are worked into the row beneath the one being worked. This creates a spike on both sides of the fabric, making the stitch ideal for reversible fabrics. You can also make spike stitches two, three, or four rows beneath the one being worked.

MATERIALS

Cascade Ultra Pima Fine
(100% pima cotton; 1.75 oz/50 g;
136.5 yds / 125 m)

Chocolate 3716 (yarn A)
Spring Green 3762 (yarn B)
Deep Coral 3767 (yarn C)

HOOK SIZE

G-6 (4 mm) crochet hook

SKILL LEVEL

Intermediate

GAUGE

Rounds 1–2 measure 1.5 in.
(4 cm), so follow pattern, and at
end of Round 2, you should have a
measurement of 1.5 in. (4 cm).

FINISHED SIZE

3.75 in. (9.5 cm) square

SPECIAL STITCHES

SDC (spike double crochet)
Yarn over the hook, insert the hook
from front to back under the top two
loops of the unworked stitch below.
Pull the yarn through the stitch and
up to the current level of work (do
not pull the yarn tight, or your work
will not lie flat). Yarn over and draw
through 2 loops on the hook twice.

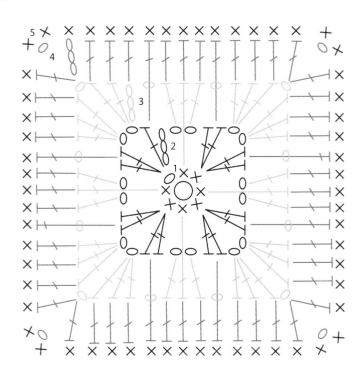

PROJECT:

Pincushion

Use scraps of yarn to make a pincushion that's too pretty to store in a sewing basket.

MATERIALS

2 squares made using Rounds 1–4 of the Retro Square motif (see left). The sample shown uses scraps of Cascade Ultra Pima Fine (100% pima cotton; 1.75 oz/50 g; 136.5 yds /125 m) in Pansy 3779 (yarn A), Primrose 3712 (yarn B), and Cool Mint 3775 (yarn C), or a similar sportweight yarn, and a C-2 (3 mm) crochet hook

Fiberfill

NOTIONS

C–2 (3 mm) crochet hook; adjust size to obtain correct gauge

GAUGE

Rounds 1–2 measure 1.5 in. (4 cm), so follow pattern, and at end of Round 2, you should have a measurement of 1.5 in. (4 cm).

FINISHED SIZE

3 in. (7.5 cm) square

INSTRUCTIONS

Using yarn A, make a magic ring.

ROUND 1 Ch1 (counts as first sc), make 7sc into ring. Join with sl st to the beg ch-1 sp. (8sc)

ROUND 2 Ch3 (counts as first dc), (1dc, ch2, 2dc) in same st, ch2, skip next st, * (2dc, ch2, 2dc) in next st, ch2, skip next st; repeat from * 2 more times. Join with sl st to the top of the beg ch-3. Fasten off.

ROUND 3 Join yarn B to any corner ch-2 sp, ch3 (counts as first dc), (2dc, ch1, 3dc) in same space, ch1, (1dc, 1SDC into skipped st from Row 1, 1dc) in next ch-2 sp, ch1, * (3dc, ch1, 3dc) in next ch-2 sp,

ch1, (1dc, 1SDC into skipped st from Row 1, 1dc) in next ch-2 sp, ch1; repeat from * 2 more times. Join with a sl st to the top of the beg ch-3. Fasten off.

ROUND 4 Join yarn C to any ch-1 corner space, ch4 (counts as 1dc, ch1), 1dc in same space, dc in each st around, making 1SDC between the 2dc from round 2 in every side ch-1 sp, and (1dc, ch1, 1dc) in every corner ch-1 sp. Join with a sl st to the 3rd ch of the beg ch4. Fasten off.

ROUND 5 Join yarn A to any st from the previous round, ch1(counts as first sc), sc in each st around. Make 2sc in each ch-1 corner sp. Join with a sl st to the first sc.

INSTRUCTIONS

Using yarn A, hold the 2 squares together RS out and join through both loops of each square; join in any ch-1 corner st from Round 4. Ch1, (1sc, ch1, 1sc) in the same space, * 1sc in the 13 sts down one side, (1sc, ch1, 1sc) in the corner ch-1 sp; repeat from * 2 more times.

Fill firmly with fiberfill and make 1sc in each of the last 13 sts. Join with a sl st to the first dc. Fasten off and weave in the ends.

Flower in a Square

The petals for this three-dimensional flower motif are made using clusters of double crochet stitches worked around a central ring. The remainder of the square is worked into the back of the petal stitches so that they stand out from the background fabric.

MATERIALS

Cascade Ultra Pima Fine
(100% pima cotton; 1.75 oz/50 g;
136.5 yds / 125 m)

Deep Coral 3767 (yarn A)
Lipstick Red 3755 (yarn B)
Natural 3718 (yarn C)
Chartreuse 3746 (yarn D)

HOOK SIZE

G-6 (4 mm) crochet hook

SKILL LEVEL

Intermediate

GAUGE

Rounds 1–2 measure 1.25 in.
(3 cm), so follow pattern, and at
end of Round 6, you should have a
measurement of 1.25 in. (3 cm).

FINISHED SIZE

3.75 in. (9.5 cm) square

INSTRUCTIONS

ROUND 1 Using yarn A, ch2, make 8sc in first ch; join with a sl st to the first sc. Fasten off. (8sc)

ROUND 2 Using yarn B, ch1; make 2sc in each st around. Join with a sl st to the first sc. (16sc)

ROUND 3 * ch2, skip next st, sl st into next st; repeat from * around. Join with a sl st to the base of the beg ch2. Fasten off. (8 ch-2 sp)

ROUND 4 Using yarn C, join in any ch-2 loop, (ch3, dc3tog, ch3, sl st) in the same loop, * sl st into the next loop, (ch3, dc3tog, ch3, sl st) in the same loop; repeat from * around. Fasten off. (8 petals)

ROUND 5 Using yarn D, and working in the back of the petals, sl st into the st between the petals, * ch2, sl st into the st between the next petal, ch3, sl st into the st between the next petal; repeat from * 3 more times, ending with a sl st into the first ch-2 loop made. (4 ch-2 loops, 4 ch-3 loops)

ROUND 6 Ch4 (counts as first 1dc, ch1), in first ch-2 loop, (3dc, ch2, 3dc, ch1) in next ch-3 loop (corner made), * 2dc, ch1 in the next ch-2 sp, (3dc, ch2, 3dc, ch1) in the next ch-3 sp; repeat from * 2 more times, 1dc in the first ch-2 sp. Join with a sl st to the top of the beg ch3.

ROUND 7 Ch3 (counts as 1dc), make 1dc in each st and each ch-1 space around; make (1dc, ch2, 1dc) in each corner ch-2 sp. Join with a sl st to the top of the beg ch3. Fasten off.

ROUND 8 Using yarn A, join in any st, ch1 (counts as first sc), sc in each st around. Make 3sc in each corner ch-2 sp. Join with a sl st to the first sc.

Circle in a Square

A combination of double and treble crochet stitches is used to create the radiating circles that form this square motif. The result is a substantial yet airy lace fabric, which suits both contrasting and complementary color schemes.

MATERIALS

Cascade Ultra Pima Fine
(100% pima cotton; 1.75 oz/50 g;
136.5 yds /125 m)

Grapeade 3816 (yarn A)
Ice 3736 (yarn B)
Primrose 3712 (yarn C)
Wood Violet 3709 (yarn D)
Natural 3718 (yarn E)

HOOK SIZE

G-6 (4 mm) crochet hook

SKILL LEVEL

Intermediate

GAUGE

Rounds 1–2 measure 2.5 in.
(6 cm), so follow pattern, and at
end of Round 2, you should have a
measurement of 2.5 in. (6 cm).

FINISHED SIZE

4.25 in. (10.75 cm) square

TRY THIS...

Use a neutral background to frame a pop of color:

Deep Coral 3767 (yarn A)
Spring Green 3762 (yarn B)
Buttercup 3748 (yarn C)
Buff 3719 (yarns D and E)

INSTRUCTIONS

Using yarn A, ch4 and sl st to join into a ring.

ROUND 1 Ch4 (counts as first dc, ch1), (1dc, ch1) 11 times into the ring. Join with a sl st to the 3rd ch of the beg ch4. Fasten off. (12dc, 12 ch-1 sp)

ROUND 2 Using yarn B, join in any ch-1 sp from Round 1. Ch3 (counts as 1dc), 1dc, ch1 into same sp, * 2dc, ch1 into next ch-1 sp; repeat from * around, join with a sl st to the top of the beg ch3. Fasten off. (24dc, 12 ch-1 sps)

ROUND 3 Using yarn C, join in any ch-1 sp from Round 2. Ch3 (counts as 1dc), 2dc, ch1 into same sp, * 3dc, ch1 into next ch-1 sp; repeat from * around. Join with a sl st to the top of the beg ch3. Fasten off. (36dc, 12 ch-1 sps)

ROUND 4 Using yarn D, join in any ch-1 sp from Round 3. Ch4 (counts as 1tr), 1tr, ch3, 2tr (corner made) into same sp, * [4dc in next ch-1 sp] twice * *, (2tr, ch3, 2tr) in next ch-1 sp; repeat from * 2 more times, and from * to * * once. Join with a sl st to the top of the beg ch4. Fasten off.

ROUND 5 Using yarn E, join to any st from Round 4. Ch1 (counts as first sc). Sc into each st around. Make (2sc, ch1, 2sc) in each corner ch3. Join with a sl st to the first sc.

MATERIALS

Rico Essentials Cotton DK (100% cotton; 1.75 oz/50 g; 142 yds/ 130 m), or a similar DK yarn

Plum 21 (yarn A) x 1 ball
Emerald 45 (yarn B) x 1 ball
Turquoise 33 (yarn C) x 1 ball
Violet 20 (yarn D) x 1 ball

NOTIONS

G-6 (4 mm) crochet hook; adjust size if necessary to obtain correct gauge

16 in. (40.5 cm) covered pillow

Matching sewing thread

Sewing needle

Tapestry needle

GAUGE

Rounds 1–2 measure 2.5 in. (6 cm), so follow pattern, and at end of Round 2, you should have a measurement of 2.5 in. (6 cm).

FINISHED SIZE

About 16.5 x 16.5 in. (42 x 42 cm)

PROJECT

Circle in a Square Square Pillow

A limited palette of calming green, blue, pink, and purple yarns creates a pool of tranquility in this pillow cover. By using the yarns in a different order for each of the sixteen squares, no two are the same—bringing a burst of color to a cozy couch or a favorite armchair. The completed pillow is finished with a border of crab stitch.

INSTRUCTIONS

Work 16 squares working Rounds 1–4 of the Circle in a Square motif (see page 50) and using different combinations of your chosen yarns.

Use a tapestry needle and scraps of yarn, which match the squares to sew the squares together to make four rows of four squares. Sew together with right sides facing, stitching through the back loops.

ROUND 1 With the right sides facing, and using yarn A, join in any corner space. Ch1 * (2sc, ch2, 2sc) (corner made), sc in each st across, 2sc in each corner sp, and 1sc in the space between squares; repeat from * until four corners and four sides have been made. Join with a sl st to the beg ch1. Fasten off.

ROUND 2 Join yarn B (or the color of your choice) in any st. Ch1, sc in each st around, and make 2sc in each corner ch-2 sp. Join with a sl st in the first sc. Fasten off.

ROUND 3 Join yarn C (or the color of your choice) in any st. Ch1, sc in each st around the four sides of the square. Join with a sl st in the first sc.

ROUND 4 Ch1, moving to the right, and make a crab st into each sc. End with a sl st into the first crab st made. Fasten off.

Pin the pillow cover to top of the pillow. Sew together using matching thread.

Lace Square

The elegant silhouettes within this lace motif are created using groups of double crochet stitches joined with a series of chain stitches and set within a double crochet border. Count the stitches carefully as you work, to ensure the motif is symmetrical.

MATERIALS

Cascade Ultra Pima Fine
(100% pima cotton; 1.75 oz/50 g;
136.5 yds / 125 m)

Turquoise 3733 (yarn A)
Natural 3718 (yarn B)

HOOK SIZE

G-6 (4 mm) crochet hook

SKILL LEVEL

Advanced

GAUGE

Rounds 1–2 measure 2 in.
(5 cm), so follow pattern, and at
end of Round 2, you should have a
measurement of 2 in. (5 cm).

FINISHED SIZE

5 in. (12.5 cm) square

INSTRUCTIONS

With yarn A, make a magic ring.

ROUND 1 Ch4 (counts as 1dc, ch1), (1dc, ch1) 7 times into ring. Join with a sl st to the 3rd ch of the beg ch4. (8dc, 8 ch–1 sps)

ROUND 2 Ch3 (counts as 1dc), make 1dc in the same st, ch2, * 2dc in the next dc, ch2; repeat from * around. Join with a sl st to the top of the beg ch3.

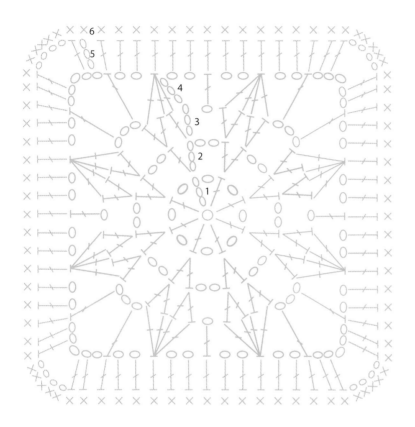

A combination of hot colors make a square that resembles a tropical flower:

China Pink 3711 (yarn A)
Coral 3752 (yarn B)
Lipstick Red 3755 (yarn C)
Chartreuse 3746 (yarn D)
Natural 3718 (yarn E)

ROUND 3 Ch3 (counts as 1dc), make 1dc in the same st, 2dc in the next tr, ch3, 2dc in each of the next 2dc, ch1 , * 2dc in each of the next 2dc, ch3, 2dc in each of the next 2dc, ch1 ; repeat from * 2 more times. Join with a sl st to the top of the beg ch3.

ROUND 4 Ch3, dc3tog over the next 3 sts, ch2, (1dc, ch5, 1dc) ch2, in the next ch-3 sp (corner made), * dc4tog over the next 4 sts, ch2, make 1dc in the ch-1 sp, ch2, dc4tog over the next 4tr, ch2, (1dc,

ch5, 1dc) ch2, in the next ch-3 sp; repeat from * 2 more times, dc4tog over the next 4dc, ch2, make 1dc in the ch-1 sp, ch2. Join with a sl st to the top of the beg ch3. Fasten off.

ROUND 5 Using yarn B, join in any ch-5 sp. Ch3 (counts as 1dc), make 1dc, ch4, make 2dc in the same space. Make 1dc in each st on the side of the square as follows: 1dc in each dc, 2dc in each ch-2 sp, 1dc on each dc4tog. (13dc). *(2dc, ch4, 2dc)

in the next ch-5 sp, make 1dc in each st on the side of the square as follows: 1dc in each dc, 2dc in each ch-2 sp, 1dc on each dc4tog; repeat from * 2 more times. Join with a sl st to the top of the beg ch3.

ROUND 6 Ch1 (counts as 1sc), make a sc in each st around, and make 5sc in each ch-4 corner sp. Join with a sl st to the first sc.

Lace Flower in a Square

Explore the versatility of chain stitches by making this floral motif, which uses chain stitches to link clusters of double and treble crochet stitches to create a flower within a square frame. A series of these joined together make a light summer shawl or lace tablecloth.

MATERIALS

Cascade Ultra Pima Fine
(100% pima cotton; 1.75 oz/50 g;
136.5 yds /125 m)

Pansy 3779 (yarn A)
Natural 3718 (yarn B)
Primrose 3712 (yarn C)
Buttercup 3748 (yarn D)
Wood Violet 3709 (yarn E)

HOOK SIZE

G-6 (4 mm) crochet hook

SKILL LEVEL

Advanced

GAUGE

Rounds 1–2 measure 1.5 in.
(4 cm), so follow pattern, and at
end of Round 2, you should have a
measurement of 1.5 in. (4 cm).

FINISHED SIZE

5.5 in. (14 cm) square

INSTRUCTIONS

Using yarn A, ch5 and join with a sl st into the ring.

ROUND 1 Ch1 (counts as first sc), make 11sc into the ring. Join with a sl st to the beg ch1. (12sc)

ROUND 2 Ch3, * 2dc in next st; repeat from * around, 1dc in base of beg ch3. Join with a sl st to the top of the beg ch3. Fasten off. (24dc)

ROUND 3 Using yarn B, join in any st, ch7 (counts as 1tr, ch3), * skip one st, 1tr in next st, ch3; repeat from * around. Join with a sl st to the 4th ch of the beg ch7. Fasten off.

ROUND 4 Using yarn C, join in any ch-3 sp, ch1, * [1sc, ch1, 1dc, 1tr, 2ch, 1tr, 1dc, ch1, 1sc] in same space; repeat from * in each ch-3 sp around. Join with a sl st in the first sc. Fasten off.

ROUND 5 Using yarn D, join in any ch-2 sp, ch1, * [1sc in ch-2 sp, ch5] 2 times, [1tr, ch5, 1tr] in next ch-2 sp, ch5. Repeat from * around; join with a sl st to the first sc.

ROUND 6 Ch1 (counts as first sc), and sc in each st around. Make 5sc in each ch-5 sp along the sides. Make 7sc in the corner ch-5 sp, and make 1sc in each sc and in each tr from the previous round. Join with a sl st into the beg ch1. Fasten off.

ROUND 7 Using yarn E, join in any st, and ch1 (counts as first sc). Sc in each st around; make 2sc in the center of the corner 7sc. Join with a sl st to the first sc.

▲▲▲ Triangles

Use a series of triangles to create simple repeating patterns that are easy on the eye and relaxing to make. Groups of these crochet shapes can be used to decorate a penholder, create an insulated pot holder, or fashion a cheerful bunting garland.

BUNTING GARLAND

There's no need to restrict bunting garlands to summer garden parties or children's birthday celebrations. Use them to bring a little extra color—and some crochet magic—to any room in the home.

For the instructions to make this design, see page 74.

Single Crochet Triangle

Working two additional single crochet stitches at each end of the row will allow you to shape this small triangle. For a larger motif, keep working rows and increasing stitches until you have the size you want. The firm fabric is ideal for joining together for patchwork designs.

MATERIALS
Cascade Ultra Pima Fine
(100% pima cotton; 1.75 oz/50 g;
136.5 yds / 125 m)

Dark Sea Foam 3797

HOOK SIZE
G-6 (4 mm) crochet hook

SKILL LEVEL
Beginner

GAUGE
Rows 1–5 measure 1 in. (2.5 cm), so follow pattern, and at end of Row 5, you should have a measurement of 1 in. (2.5 cm).

FINISHED SIZE
2.25 in. (5.5 cm) long

INSTRUCTIONS

ROW 1 Ch2, make 2sc in the 2nd ch from the hook, turn. (2sc)

ROW 2 Ch1, make 2sc in the first st, make 1sc in 2nd st, turn. (3sc)

ROW 3 Ch1, make 2sc in the first st, make 1sc in each of the next 2 sts, turn. (4sc)

ROW 4 Ch1, make 2sc in the first st, make 1sc in each st to the end, turn. (5sc)

ROWS 5 – 11 Repeat Row 4. (12sc)
Fasten off and weave in the ends.

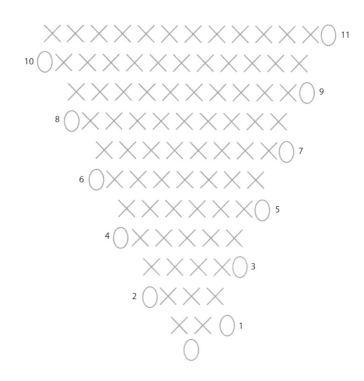

TRY THESE...

Make triangles from calming shades and join them together to make a patchwork of crochet shapes:

Coral 3752

MATERIALS

Cascade Ultra Pima Fine (100% pima cotton; 1.75 oz/50 g; 136.5 yds / 125 m), or a similar sportweight yarn

Coral 3752 (yarn A) x 1 ball
Deep Coral 3767 (yarn B) x 1 ball
Jade 3735 (yarn C) x 1 ball
Cool Mint 3775 (yarn D) x 1 ball

Glass jar or container measuring 10 in. (25.5 cm) in circumference and 6 in. (15 cm) high

NOTIONS

E-4 (3.5 mm) crochet hook; adjust size if necessary to obtain correct gauge

Tapestry needle

GAUGE

Rows 1–5 measure 1 in. (2.5 cm), so follow pattern, and at end of Row 5, you should have a measurement of 1 in. (2.5 cm).

FINISHED SIZE

Measures 10 in (25.5 cm) in circumference and approx 6 in. (15 cm) in height.

PROJECT

Penholder

Small motifs like these triangles are quick and satisfying to make, making them perfect for days when you need a few minutes of crochet to help you to unwind. This useful holder is ideal for crochet hooks as well as paintbrushes and pens. You can adjust the number of triangles or the depth of the border to suit the dimensions of your jar.

INSTRUCTIONS

Make 12 triangles by working Rows 1–11 of the Single Crochet Triangle motif (see page 60), but do not fasten off the yarn at the end of Row 11. You will then begin working down the first side of the triangle to make a sc row around 2 sides of the triangle.

ROUND 12 Ch1, make 1sc in each row end to the tip of the triangle (11sc), make 3sc in the st at the tip of the triangle, make 1sc in each row end of the 2nd side of the triangle (11sc). Join with a sl st to the first sc in the top row. Fasten off.

Make 12 triangles in all, 3 in yarn A, 3 in yarn B, 3 in yarn C, and 3 in yarn D.

FINISHING

Pin and steam block each triangle into shape.

Arrange the motifs in 2 rows of 6 triangles following the arrangement shown in the picture. Join by holding each piece with the RS together and whipstitch using the back loops only. When you have 2 rows joined, form the piece into a circle and use a whipstitch to join the first and last triangles together.

EDGING

ROW 1 Join yarn C in any stitch on top of the piece. Ch1, and make1sc evenly in each st around. Join with a sl st to the first sc made. Fasten off.

ROWS 2 AND 3 Repeat Row 1 with yarn A and yarn C. Finish using an invisible join. Repeat Rows 1–3 for the bottom of the piece.

Double Crochet Triangle

Get comfortable with increasing double crochet stitches at the end of the rows by working this simple triangle with a single crochet border.

MATERIALS

Cascade Ultra Pima Fine (100% pima cotton; 1.75 oz/50 g; 136.5 yds / 125 m)

Lavender 3778

HOOK SIZE

G-6 (4 mm) crochet hook

SKILL LEVEL

Beginner

GAUGE

Rows 1–4 measure 2 in. (5 cm), so follow pattern, and at end of Row 4, you should have a measurement of 2 in. (5 cm).

FINISHED SIZE

6.25 in. (15.5 cm) long

INSTRUCTIONS

ROW 1 Ch4, make 2dc into the first chain, turn. (3 dc)

ROW 2 Ch3, make 1dc into the first st, make 1dc into the next st, make 2dc into the t-ch. (5 dc)

ROW 3 Ch3, make 1dc into the first st. Make 1dc into each st across, make 2dc into the t-ch. (7dc)

ROWS 4–12 Repeat Row 3. (25 dc) Do not break off the yarn.

BORDER

Ch1 and sc evenly down the side of the triangle, making 2sc into each dc row. Make 3sc at the tip of the triangle and sc evenly along the opposite side. Make 2sc into

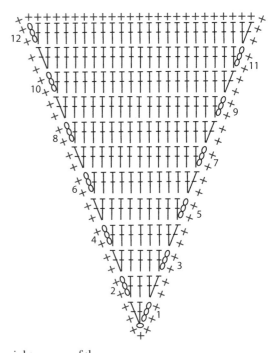

the top right corner of the triangle and make 1sc into each st along the top. Make 2sc into the top left side and join with a sl st into the first sc made. Fasten off and weave in the ends.

Circle in Triangle

A sunburst of double crochet and chain stitches
are worked in rounds to form this motif.

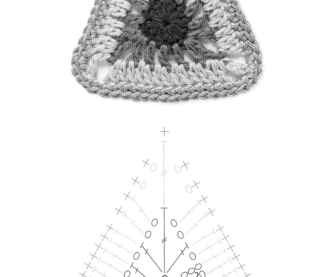

MATERIALS

Cascade Ultra Pima Fine
(100% pima cotton;
1.75 oz/50 g;
136.5 yds /125 m)

Lipstick Red 3755 (yarn A)
Deep Coral 3767 (yarn B)
Buttercup 3748 (yarn C)
Taupe 3759 (yarn D)

HOOK SIZE

G-6 (4 mm) crochet hook

SKILL LEVEL

Beginner

GAUGE

Rounds 1–2 measure 2.25
in. (5.75 cm) at the widest
point, so follow pattern,
and at end of Round 2, you
should have a measurement
of 2.25 in. (5.75 cm) at the
widest point.

FINISHED SIZE

4 in. (10 cm) long

INSTRUCTIONS

Using yarn A, make a magic
ring.

ROUND 1 Ch3 (counts as
1dc) and make 11dc into the
ring. Join with a sl st to the
top of the beg ch3. Fasten off.
(12 dc)

ROUND 2 Join yarn B to any
st. Ch4 (counts as 1dc, ch1)
* (1dc, ch2, 1tr, ch2, 1dc,
ch1) in the next st, (1dc, ch1)
in the next 3 sts; repeat from
* 1 more time, (1dc, ch2, 1tr,
ch2, 1dc, ch1) in the next st,
* (1dc, ch1) in the next 2 sts.
Join with a sl st to the 3rd ch of
the beg ch4. Fasten off.

ROUND 3 Join yarn C to the
top of any tr st from Round 2.
Ch6 (counts as 1tr, ch2), *
2dc in the next ch-2 sp, (1dc
in the next dc, 1dc in the ch-1

sp) 4 times, make 1dc in the
next dc, 2dc in the ch-2 sp,
ch2, ** 1tr in the next tr, ch2;
repeat from * once more, and
from * to ** once more. Join
with sl st to 4th ch of the beg
ch6. Fasten off.

ROUND 4 Join yarn D to the
top of any tr st from Round 3.

Ch1 (does not count as sc),
1sc in the same st, make 2sc in
the next ch-2 sp, 1sc in each of
the next 13 sts, 2sc in the next
ch-2 sp, * 1sc in the tr, 2sc in
the next ch-2 sp, 1sc in each of
the next 13 sts, 2sc in the next
ch-2 sp; repeat from * once
more. Join with a sl st to the
first sc. Fasten off.

Pot Holder

Making household items such as pot holders is doubly satisfying: You can destress as you stitch and you will be able to use the finished object every day. The double layer of shapes made using a thick cotton yarn ensures a good level of insulation.

MATERIALS

Rico Creative Cotton Aran (100% cotton; 1.75 oz/50 g; 92 yds/84 m), or a similar worsted weight yarn

Sky Blue 37 (yarn A) x 1 ball
Cherry 65 (yarn B) x 1 ball
Mustard 70 (yarn C) x 1 ball

NOTIONS

Size 7 (4.5 mm) crochet hook; adjust size if necessary to obtain correct gauge

Tapestry needle

GAUGE

Circle in a Triangle: Rounds 1–2 measure 2.75 in. (7 cm) at the widest point, so follow pattern, and at end of Round 2 you should have a measurement of 2.75 in. (7 cm). Double Crochet Triangle: Rows 1–4 measure 2 in. (5 cm).

FINISHED SIZE

Pot holder measures 10 in (25.5 cm) in diameter

INSTRUCTIONS

FRONT

Make 3 triangles using the Circle in a Triangle motif (see page 65) and using the following colors:
Round 1: Yarn A.
Round 2: Yarn C.
Round 3: Yarn B.

Using the Circle in a Triangle motif, make 3 triangles using the following colors:
Round 1: Yarn B.
Round 2: Yarn C.
Round 3: Yarn A.

Using Round 1 of the Circle in a Triangle motif and yarn C, make a circle.

BACK

Using Rows 1–8 of the Double Crochet Triangle motif (see page 64), make 2 triangles in yarn A, 2 triangles in yarn B, and 2 triangles in yarn C.

FINISHING

Pin and steam block each triangle into shape.

For the front of the pot holder, arrange the six Circle in a Triangle motifs in a hexagon shape following the arrangement shown in the photograph (right). Join by holding each piece with the RS together and whipstitch using the back loops only. Sew a small circle using yarn C to the center of the front piece.

For the back of the pot holder, arrange the six Double Crochet Triangle motifs in a hexagon shape in the following order: yarn A, yarn B, yarn C, yarn A, yarn B, and yarn C. Join by evenly whipstitching along the sides of the triangles.

BORDER

Holding the 2 pieces with the WS together, and the front of the pot holder facing, join the two pieces by making a sc edging, working through both pieces. Join yarn C in the right-hand corner of any triangle. Ch1, make 1sc in the same st, make 1sc in each st (through both layers), including the ch-2 sp, to the first corner, make 2sc in the corner. Repeat around, working as evenly as you can, until you reach the first sc. Ch15, sl st into the first ch (hanging loop made), and join with a sl st into the first sc made. Fasten off.

Solid Triangle

Neat rounds of double crochet stitches form a dense triangle motif that enhances a bold color scheme. Groups of stitches worked around a central circle create the triangle shape. The hot red and bright yellow create a burst of color when used with the blue and green shades.

MATERIALS

Cascade Ultra Pima Fine
(100% pima cotton; 1.75 oz/50 g;
136.5 yds /125 m)

Lipstick Red 3755 (yarn A)
Chartreuse 3746 (yarn B)
Teal 3734 (yarn C)
Cool Mint 3775 (yarn D)
Wood Violet 3709 (yarn E)

HOOK SIZE

G-6 (4 mm) crochet hook

SKILL LEVEL

Beginner

GAUGE

Rounds 1–2 measure 2 in. (5 cm),
so follow pattern, and at end
of Round 2, you should have a
measurement of 2 in. (5 cm).

FINISHED SIZE

5.25 in. (13 cm) long

INSTRUCTIONS

Using yarn A, ch4 and join in a ring.

ROUND 1 Ch3 (counts as 1dc) and make 14dc into the ring. Join with a sl st to the top of the beg ch3. Fasten off. (15 dc)

TRY THIS...

A dark center surrounded by rounds of pale colors creates a focal point:

Teal 3734 (yarn A in first round)

Dark Sea Foam 3797 (yarn B)

Sage 3720 (yarn C)

Natural 3718 (yarn D)

Coral 3752 (yarn A in fifth round)

Yellow Rose 3743 (yarn E)

ROUND 2 Join yarn B in any st. Ch3 (counts as 1dc), (1dc, ch1, 2dc) in the same st, make 1dc in each of the next 4 sts, * (2dc, ch1, 2dc) in the next st, make 1dc in each of the next 4 sts; repeat from * once more. Join with a sl st to top of the beg ch3. Fasten off.

ROUND 3 Join yarn C in any ch-1 corner sp. Ch3 (counts as 1dc), (1dc, ch1, 2dc) in the same space, make 1hdc in each of the next 2 sts, make 1sc in each of the next 4 sts, make 1hdc in each of next 2 sts, * (2dc, ch1, 2dc) in the next ch-1 sp, make 1hdc in each of the next 2 sts, make 1sc in each of the next 4 sts, make 1hdc in each of the next 2 sts; repeat from * once more. Join with a sl st to the top of the beg ch3. Fasten off.

ROUND 4 Join yarn D in any ch-1 corner sp. Ch3 (counts as 1dc), (1dc, ch1, 2dc) in the same space, make 1dc in each of the next 12 sts, * (2dc, ch1, 2dc) in the next ch-1 sp, make 1dc in each of the next 12 sts; repeat from * once more. Join with a sl st to top of the beg ch3. Fasten off.

ROUND 5 Join yarn A in any ch-1 corner sp. Ch3 (counts as 1dc), (1dc, ch2, 2dc) in the same space, make 1dc in each of the next 16 sts, * (2dc, ch2, 2dc) in the next ch-1 sp, make 1dc in each of the next 16 sts; repeat from * once more. Join with a sl st to the top of beg ch3. Fasten off .

ROUND 6 Join yarn E in any st. Ch1 (does not count as sc), make 1sc in the next and every st around, making 3sc in each corner ch-2 sp. Join with a sl st to the first sc. Weave in the ends.

Bold Flower Triangle

A five-petal double crochet flower sits at the heart of this triangle motif and contrasting colored yarns make it the star of the show. To enhance it, you can work the border in a single color or you can create a series of stripes to really set it off.

MATERIALS

Cascade Ultra Pima Fine
(100% pima cotton; 1.75 oz/50 g;
136.5 yds /125 m)

Lipstick Red 3755 (yarn A)
Natural 3718 (yarn B)

HOOK SIZE

G-6 (4 mm) crochet hook

SKILL LEVEL

Intermediate

GAUGE

Rounds 1–2 measure 2.25 in.
(5.75 cm) at the widest point, so
follow pattern, and at end of Round
2, you should have a measurement
of 2.25 in. (5.75 cm) at the widest
point.

FINISHED SIZE

4 in. (10 cm) long

INSTRUCTIONS
Make a magic ring.

ROUND 1 Using yarn A, ch3 and make dc2tog in the ring (counts as dc3tog). Ch5, * dc3tog, ch3, dc3tog, ch5; repeat from * once more, dc3tog, ch3. Join with a sl st to the top of the beg cluster. Fasten off. (6 cl, 3 ch-3 sps, 3 ch-5 sps)

ROUND 2 Join yarn B in any ch-3 sp and ch1, 1sc, 1hdc in the same space, make 1hdc in the next cl, * (3dc, 1tr, 3dc) in the next ch-5 sp, make 1hdc in the next cl, ** (1hdc, 1sc, 1hdc) in the next ch-3 sp, make1hdc in the next cl; repeat from * once more and from * to ** once more. Make 1hdc in the next ch-3 sp. Join with a sl st to the first hdc.

ROUND 3 Ch3 (counts as 1dc), * 1dc in each st to the corner, (2dc, ch2, 2dc) in the corner tr st; repeat from * 2 more times and make 1dc in each of the next 6 sts. Join with a sl st to the top of the beg ch3. Fasten off.

ROUND 4 Join yarn A in any stitch. Ch1 and make 1sc in each st around, making 3sc in each corner ch-2 sp. Join with a sl st to the first sc. Fasten off.

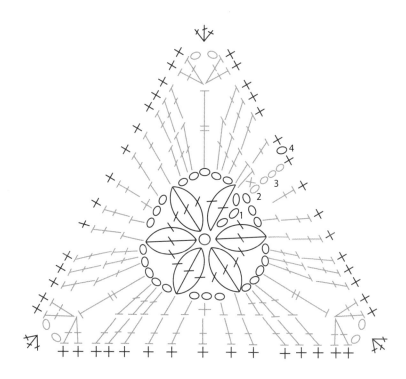

Framed Circle Triangle

A simple central circle is joined by lace-like double crochet stitches to a double crochet border. Start with dense rounds of double crochet stitches in a selection of complementary colors and then add a round of bright, contrasting single crochet stitches for a pop of color.

MATERIALS

Cascade Ultra Pima Fine
(100% pima cotton; 1.75 oz/50 g;
136.5 yds /125 m)

Lavender 3778 (yarn A)
Chartreuse 3746 (yarn B)
Delphinium 3706 (yarn C)
Pansy 3779 (yarn D)

HOOK SIZE

G-6 (4 mm) crochet hook

SKILL LEVEL

Intermediate

GAUGE

Rounds 1–2 measure 1.5 in.
(4 cm), so follow pattern, and at
end of Round 2, you should have a
measurement of 1.5 in. (4 cm).

FINISHED SIZE

4 in. (10 cm) long

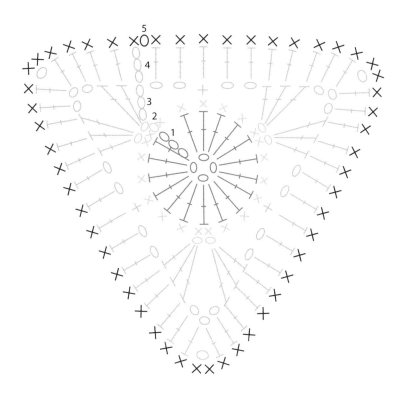

TRY THIS...

A ring of pink stitches bring a pop of color to a collection of cool greens and gray:

Cool Mint 3775 (yarn A)
Primrose 3712 (yarn B)
Ice 3736 (yarn C)
Gray 3729 (yarn D)

INSTRUCTIONS

Using yarn A, ch4 and join with sl st in a ring.

ROUND 1 Ch3 (counts as 1dc) and make 17dc in the ring. Join with sl st to the top of the beg ch3. Fasten off. (18 dc)

ROUND 2 Using yarn B, join in any st. Ch1, (1sc, ch2, 1sc) in the same st, * 1sc in each of the next 5 sts, (1sc, ch2, 1sc) in the next st; repeat from * once more. Make 1sc in each of the next 5 sts. Join with a sl st to the first sc. Fasten off.

ROUND 3 Using yarn C, join in any ch-2 sp. Ch3 (counts as 1dc), (2dc, ch3, 3dc) in the same space, * ch2, skip 2 sts, make1sc in the next st, ch2, skip 2 sts, * * (3dc, ch3, 3dc) in the next ch-2 sp; repeat from * once more and from * to * * once. Join with a sl st to the top of the beg ch3. Do not fasten off.

ROUND 4 Ch3 (counts as 1dc), make1dc in the next 2 sts, * (2dc, ch1, 2dc) in the next ch-3 sp, make 1dc in each of the next 3 sts, make 2dc in the next ch-2 sp, make 1dc in the next sc, make 2dc in the next ch-2 sp, * * 3dc in each of the next 3 sts; repeat from * once more and from * to * * once. Join with a sl st to the top of the beg ch3. Fasten off.

ROUND 5 Join yarn D in any st. Ch1, make 1sc in the next st and each st around, making 2sc in each ch-1 sp. Join with a sl st to the first sc. Fasten off and weave in the ends.

Dainty Flower Triangle

Rounds of double crochet and double crochet clusters create a frame for the simple double crochet flower that's placed at the center of this triangle. Use rounds of contrasting colors to create impact or choose cool pastels for a classic finish.

MATERIALS

Cascade Ultra Pima Fine
(100% pima cotton; 1.75 oz/50 g;
136.5 yds / 125 m)

Coral 3752 (yarn A)
Ice 3736 (yarn B)
Deep Coral 3767 (yarn C)
Chartreuse 3746 (yarn D)

HOOK SIZE

G-6 (4 mm) crochet hook

SKILL LEVEL

Intermediate

GAUGE

Rounds 1–2 measure 2 in.
(5 cm), so follow pattern, and at
end of Round 2, you should have a
measurement of 2 in. (5 cm).

FINISHED SIZE

5.75 in. (14.5 cm) long

INSTRUCTIONS

Using yarn A, make a magic ring.

ROUND 1 Ch3 (counts as 1dc) and make 11dc in the ring. Join with a sl st to the top of the beg ch3. Fasten off. (12dc)

ROUND 2 Using yarn B, join in any st. Ch1, (1sc in the same st, skip 1 st, ch5),

Bunting Garland

These colorful flags bring a burst of color to a child's bedroom or vintage charm to a party.

MATERIALS

7 triangles made using Rounds 1–4 of the Dainty Flower Triangle motif (see left). The sample shown uses different combinations of Rico Creative Cotton Aran (100% cotton; 1.75 oz/50 g; 92 yds/84 m) in Sky Blue 37 (yarn A), Petrol 47 (yarn B), Cherry 65 (yarn C), Mustard 70 (yarn D), and a size 7 (4.5 mm) crochet hook, or a similar worsted weight yarn

NOTIONS

Size 7 (4.5 mm) crochet hook; adjust size if necessary to obtain correct gauge

GAUGE

1 triangle measures 5.5 in. (14 cm) long

FINISHED SIZE

Garland is approx 60 in. (152.5 cm) long

INSTRUCTIONS

ROUND 5 Ch1, make 1sc in each st around, and make (1sc, ch2, 1sc) in each corner sp. Fasten off. Pin and steam block into shape.

FINISHING Join the triangles as follows : Using yarn A, ch20, sl st into the first ch to form a hanging loop and ch10. Holding the first triangle with the RS in front, make 1sc in the ch-2 corner sp, make 1sc in each st across, make 1sc in the next ch-2 corner sp. * Taking the next triangle, make 1sc in the ch-2 corner sp, make 1sc in each st across, make 1sc in the next ch-2 corner sp; repeat from * until all the triangles are attached. Ch30, sl st into the 20th st made to form a hanging loop, fasten off, and weave in the ends.

---

* (1sc in next st, skip 1 st, ch5) repeat from * 4 times. Join with a sl st into the first sc. (6 ch-5 lps)

ROUND 3 Sl st into the next ch-5 sp, (ch3, dc2tog, ch3, tr3tog, ch3, dc3tog) in the same space, ch3, * 1sc in the next ch-5 sp, ch3, (dc3tog, ch3, tr3tog, ch3, dc3tog) in the next ch-5 sp, ch3; repeat from * once more; make 1sc in the next ch-5 sp, ch3. Join with a sl st to the top of the first dc2tog cl. Fasten off.

ROUND 4 Using yarn C, join in the top of the tr3tog cl. Ch6 (counts as 1dc, ch3), make 2dc in the same st, * 3dc in the next ch-3 sp, make 1dc in the next st (top of dc3tog cl), (3dc in next ch-3 sp, 1dc in the next st) twice, make 3dc in the next ch-3 sp, ** (2dc, ch3, 2dc) in the next st (top of tr3tog cl); repeat from * once more and from * to ** once; make 1dc in the next st (beg tr3tog cl). Join with a sl st to the 3rd ch of the beg ch6. Fasten off.

ROUND 5 Join yarn D in a corner ch-3 sp. Ch6 (counts as 1dc, ch3), make 2dc in the same space, * 1dc in each of the 19 sts across to the next corner, ** (2dc, ch3, 2dc) in the ch-3 sp; repeat from * once more and from * to ** once. Make 1dc in the next ch-3 sp. Join with a sl st to 3rd ch of the beg ch6. Fasten off and weave in the ends.

Lace Flower Triangle

A generously sized bloom sits at the center of this pretty lace triangle. The substantial double crochet center and petals are joined to the double crochet border by a series of single and groups of treble crochet stitches for a delicate finished motif.

MATERIALS

Cascade Ultra Pima Fine (100% pima cotton; 1.75 oz/50 g; 136.5 yds / 125 m)

Cool Mint 3775 (yarn A)
Primrose 3712 (yarn B)
Natural 3718 (yarn C)
Ice 3736 (yarn D)

HOOK SIZE

G-6 (4 mm) crochet hook

SKILL LEVEL

Advanced

GAUGE

Rounds 1–3 measure 2.75 in. (7 cm), so follow pattern, and at end of Round 2, you should have a measurement of 2.75 in. (7 cm).

FINISHED SIZE

5.75 in. (14.5 cm) long

INSTRUCTIONS

Using yarn A, ch4 and join in a ring.

ROUND 1 Ch4 (counts as 1dc, ch1) and work (1dc, ch1) 11 times into the ring. Join with a sl st to 3rd ch of the beg ch4. Fasten off.

ROUND 2 Using yarn B, join in any ch-1 sp. Ch1, make 1sc in same space, * ch4, tr4tog in the next ch-1 sp, ch4, ** make 1sc in the next ch-1 sp; repeat from * 4 more times, then from * to ** once. Join with a sl st in the first sc made. Fasten off. (6 tr4tog clusters)

ROUND 3 Using yarn C, join in the top of any tr4tog cluster. Ch1, * 1sc in the top of the tr4tog cl, ch2, make 1tr in the next sc (from Round 2), ch2, (3tr, ch4, 3tr) in the top of the next tr4tog cl, ch2, make 1tr in the next sc, ch2; repeat from * 2 more times. Join with a sl st to the first sc. Fasten off.

ROUND 4 Join yarn D in any ch-4 sp. Ch3 (counts as 1dc), (2dc, ch4, 3dc) in the same space, * 1dc in each of the next 3 sts, (2dc in the next ch-2 sp, 1dc in the next st) 3 times, 2dc in the ch-2 sp, 1dc in each of the next 3 sts, ** (3dc, ch4, 3dc) in the next ch-4 sp; repeat from * 1 more time and from * to ** once more. Join with a sl st to the first tr. Fasten off.

TRY THIS...

Bright colors bring a summery vibe to this lace motif:

Chocolate 3716 (yarn A)
Tangerine 3750 (yarn B)
Wood Violet 3709 (yarn C)
Buttercup 3748 (yarn D)

Windflower Triangle

The delicate chain stitch petals at the center of this triangle appear to be blown by the breeze. Once worked, additional lengths of chain stitches join the petals to a double crochet border, which holds them securely in place. Bold colors add to the impact of this motif.

MATERIALS

Cascade Ultra Pima Fine (100% pima cotton; 1.75 oz/50 g; 136.5 yds / 125 m)

Deep Coral 3767 (yarn A)
Teal 3734 (yarn B)
Wood Violet 3709 (yarn C)

HOOK SIZE

G-6 (4 mm) crochet hook

SKILL LEVEL

Advanced

GAUGE

Rounds 1–2 measure 2.25 in. (5.75 cm), so follow pattern, and at end of Round 2, you should have a measurement of 2.25 in. (5.75 cm).

FINISHED SIZE

5.5 in. (14 cm) long

INSTRUCTIONS

Using yarn A, make a magic ring.

ROUND 1 Ch1 and make 9sc into the ring. Join with a sl st to the first sc. (9sc)

ROUND 2 Ch1 and make 1sc in the first sc, * ch9, make 1sc in the next st; repeat from * 7 times, ch9. Join with a sl st to the first sc. Fasten off. (9 ch lps)

ROUND 3 Using yarn B, join in any ch-9 sp. Ch1 and make 1sc in the same space, * (ch5, make 1sc in the next ch9 sp) twice, ch10, sl st back into the 7th ch from the hook, ch2 (corner made), ** make 1sc in the next ch-9 sp; repeat from * once more, then from * to ** once. Join with a sl st to the first sc. Fasten off.

ROUND 4 Using yarn C, join the yarn in a ch-5 sp to the left of the corner ch-7 sp. Ch1 and make 1sc in the same space, * ch5, make 1sc in the next ch-5 sp, ch5, (1sc, ch5, 1sc) in the next ch-7 sp, ch5, ** make 1sc in the next ch-5 sp; repeat from * once more, then from * to ** once. Join with a sl st to the first sc made.

ROUND 5 Ch3 (counts as 1dc), * 5dc in the next ch-5 sp, make 1dc in the next sc, make 5dc in the next ch-5 sp, make 1dc in the next sc, make 7dc in the next ch-5 sp (corner), make 1dc in the next sc, make 5dc in the next ch-5 sp **, make 1dc in the next sc; repeat from * once and from * to ** once more. Join with a sl st to the top of the beg ch3. Fasten off and weave in the ends.

Edelweiss Triangle

A delicate flower is suspended within a framework of chain stitches for this lace motif. The lace is joined to the central flower using slip stitches and is bordered by rounds of chains, which form a grid-like lace between the flower and double and single crochet border.

MATERIALS

Cascade Ultra Pima Fine
(100% pima cotton; 1.75 oz/50 g;
136.5 yds /125 m)

Sand 3717 (yarn A)
Buttercup 3748 (yarn B)
Natural 3718 (yarn C)
Spring Green 3762 (yarn D)

HOOK SIZE

G-6 (4 mm) crochet hook

SKILL LEVEL

Advanced

GAUGE

Rounds 1–3 measure 2.5 in.
(6 cm), so follow pattern, and at
end of Round 3, you should have a
measurement of 2.5 in. (6 cm).

FINISHED SIZE

6.5 in. (16.5 cm) long

INSTRUCTIONS

ROUND 1 Using yarn A, ch2 and make 6sc into the 2nd ch from the hook. Fasten off. (6sc)

ROUND 2 Using yarn B, join in any sc; (ch4, tr2tog, ch4) in the same st, sl st into the next st, * (ch4, tr2tog, ch4), sl st into the next st; repeat from * 4 more times, ending with a sl st into the first ch of the beg ch4. Fasten off.

ROUND 3 Using yarn C, join in the top of a tr2tog cl. Ch1 and make 1sc in the same st, * ch5, make 1sc in the top of the next tr2tog cl, ch11, ** make1sc in the top of the next tr2tog cl; repeat from * once more, then from * to ** once. Join with a sl st to the first sc. Do not fasten off.

ROUND 4 Ch6 (counts as 1dc, ch3), make 1dc in the next ch-5 sp, ch3, make 1dc in the next sc, * (ch3, 1dc, ch3, 1dc, ch5, 1dc, ch3, 1dc, ch3) in the next ch11 sp, ** 1dc in the next sc, ch3, make 1dc in the next ch-5 sp, ch3, make 1dc in the next sc; repeat from * once more and from * to ** once. Join with a sl st to the 3rd ch of the beg ch6.

ROUND 5 Sl st in the next ch-3 sp, ch3 (counts as 1dc), make 2dc in the same sp,

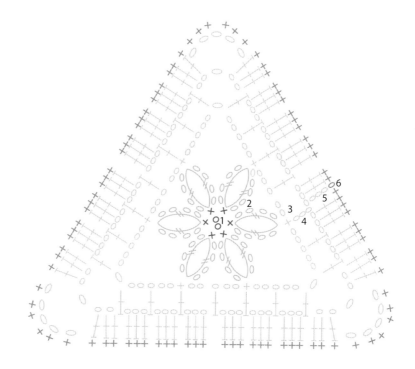

(3dc in the next ch-3 sp) 3 times, * (3dc, ch5, 3dc) in the next ch-5 sp, ** (3dc in the next ch-3 sp) 6 times; repeat from * once more and from * to ** once, (3dc in the next ch-3 sp) twice. Join with a sl st to the top of the beg ch3. Fasten off.

ROUND 6 Using yarn D, join in any st. Ch1 and make 1sc in the next and each st around, making 6sc in each corner ch-5 sp. Join with a sl st to the first sc. Fasten off and weave in the ends.

TRY THIS...

Use a contemporary color palette to transform this vintage motif:

Teal 3734 (yarn A)
Primrose 3712 (yarn B)
Dark Sea Foam 3797 (yarn C)
Magenta 3703 (yarn D)

Stripes

Simple, soothing stripes of color are a cinch to crochet and rely on combinations of stitches to add texture to a design. Use them to create a holder for your tablet device, a hat to wear on a cold day, or a blanket to celebrate a new life.

TABLET COZY

Protect your tablet from knocks and scratches by storing it in a custom-made sleeve. This pattern can be used to cover any size of device so you can crochet a smaller version for your cell phone, too. For the instructions to make this design, see page 92.

Granny Stripes

Like its Granny Square relative (see page 34), the Granny Stripe is simple to learn and quickly works up into a substantial and decorative fabric. For this sample, we used the same neutral color for the odd-numbered rows and a series of contrasting colors for the even rows. But why not try it using just two colors, or even a whole rainbow?

MATERIALS

Cascade Ultra Pima Fine
(100% pima cotton; 1.75 oz/50 g;
136.5 yds /125 m)

Natural 3718 (yarn A)
Ice 3736 (yarn B)
Delphinium 3706 (yarn C)
Cool Mint 3775 (yarn D)
Sand 3717 (yarn E)
Wood Violet 3709 (yarn F)

HOOK SIZE

G-6 (4 mm) crochet hook

SKILL LEVEL

Beginner

GAUGE

6 groups of 3dc in pattern x 11 rows
= 4 in. (10 cm) square

FINISHED SIZE

4.5 x 5.75 in. (11.5 x 14.5 cm)

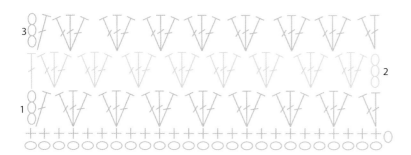

INSTRUCTIONS

Work a chain of a multiple of 3 sts plus 2 for the Foundation Row.

FOUNDATION ROW With yarn A, make 1sc in the 2nd ch from hook, and 1sc in each ch to the end, turn.

ROW 1 Ch3 (counts as 1dc), make 1dc in first st, * skip next 2 sts, make 3dc in next st; repeat from * ending with 2dc in the last st. Change to yarn B, turn.

ROW 2 Ch3 (counts as 1dc), *3dc into the next sp (between 2 clusters); repeat from * ending with 1dc into the top sp of the t-ch. Change to Yarn A, turn.

ROW 3 Ch3 (counts as 1dc), 1dc in same st, * 3dc into the next sp; repeat from * ending with 2dc in the top sp of the t-ch. Change to yarn C, turn.

TO WORK THE PATTERN

Repeat Rows 2 and 3, changing color at the end of each row as follows:

Row 4: Change to yarn A.
Row 5: Change to yarn D.
Row 6: Change to yarn A.
Row 7: Change to yarn E.
Row 8: Change to yarn A.
Row 9: Change to yarn F.
Row 10: Change to yarn A.

TRY THIS...

Bright colors provide a contrast to stripes of bold red stitches:

Magenta 3703 (yarn A on Rows 1 and 11, yarn D on Row 6)

Aqua 3732 (yarn B on Row 2, yarn A on row 7)

Primrose 3712 (yarn A on Row 3, yarn E on Row 8)

Chartreuse 3746 (yarn A on Row 9, yarn C on Row 4)

Tangerine 3750 (yarn A on Row 5, yarn F on Row 10)

Half Double Crochet Stripe

By changing the color of yarn for every row of these half double crochet stitch stripes, the colors intertwine to create interlocking stripes. For more solid stripes, change the yarn color every two rows. This stripe sequence provides plenty of opportunity to experiment with color.

MATERIALS
Cascade Ultra Pima Fine (100% pima cotton; 1.75 oz/50 g; 136.5 yds /125 m) in several colors

HOOK SIZE
G-6 (4 mm) crochet hook

SKILL LEVEL
Beginner

GAUGE
18hdc x 13 rows = 4 in. (10 cm) square

FINISHED SIZE
4.5 x 5.25 in. (11.5 x 13 cm)

INSTRUCTIONS
Work a chain of any number of stitches, plus 2 for the Foundation Row.

FOUNDATION ROW Make 1hdc in the 3rd ch from the hook, and make 1hdc in each ch to the end, turn.

ROW 1 Ch2 (counts as 1hdc), skip first st. Make 1hdc in each st to the end. Make the last hdc in the t-ch of the previous row.

TO WORK THE PATTERN
Repeat Row 1, changing the color of the yarn as required.

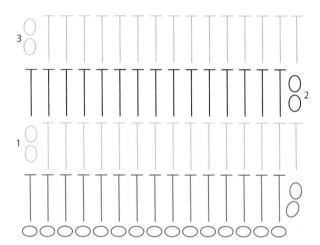

Cross Hatch Stripes

Groups of three double crochet stitches worked at a forty-five-degree angle to the row beneath them, create geometric waves of contrasting color. This stitch is a simple way to create interesting textures by repeating two rows of the pattern.

MATERIALS

Cascade Ultra Pima Fine (100% pima cotton; 1.75 oz/50 g; 136.5 yds /125 m)

Lavender 3778 (yarn A)
Primrose 3712 (yarn B)
Buttercup 3748 (yarn C)
Magenta 3703 (yarn D)

HOOK SIZE

G-6 (4 mm) crochet hook

SKILL LEVEL

Beginner

GAUGE

4 groups of 3dc in pattern x 10 rows = 4 in. (10 cm) square

FINISHED SIZE

5 x 5.5 in. (12.5 x 14 cm)

INSTRUCTIONS

Work a chain of a multiple of 7 sts for the Foundation Row.

FOUNDATION ROW Using yarn A, make 2dc in the 3rd chain from the hook (counts as 3dc), * skip the next 3 ch, make 1sc in the next ch, ch3, make 1dc in each of the next 3 chs; repeat from * to last 4 chs, skip next 3 chs. Make 1sc in the last ch. Fasten off, turn.

ROW 1 Using yarn B, ch3 (counts as 1dc), make 2dc in first sc; * skip next 3dc. Make 1sc in the first ch, ch3; make 1dc in each of the next 2 chs, make 1dc in the next sc; repeat from *. End by skipping the last 2dc; make 1sc in the top of the t-ch. Fasten off, turn.

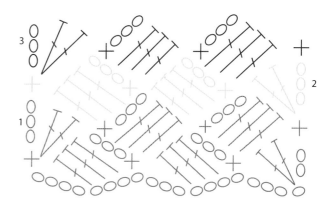

TO WORK THE PATTERN

Repeat Row 1, working the stripes as follows:

Row 2: Yarn C.
Row 3: Yarn D.
Row 4: Yarn A.
Row 5: Yarn B.
Row 6: Yarn C.
Row 7: Yarn D.
Row 8: Yarn A.
Row 9: Yarn B.
Row 10: Yarn C.
Row 11: Yarn D.

Child's Hat

Groups of double crochet stitches combine to create a mosaic of squares that are easy to memorize, deceptively simple to make, and a perfect way to help you to unwind. This hat requires no shaping —simply make a rectangle, then use a length of yarn to gather the fabric at one end to close the crown. It is finished with a single crochet border and a fluffy pompom.

MATERIALS

Cascade Pacific Yarn (60% acrylic, 40% Merino wool; 3/5 oz/100 g; 213 yds/195 m), or a similar worsted weight yarn

Almond 60 (yarn A) x 1 ball
Cream 01 (yarn B) x 1 ball
Peacock 40 (yarn C) x 1 ball
Dusty Turquoise 23 (yarn D) x 1 ball
Yellow 12 (yarn E) x 1 ball

NOTIONS

Size 7 (4.5 mm) and H-8 (5 mm) crochet hooks; adjust size if necessary to obtain correct gauge

Tapestry needle

Cardboard or pompom maker

GAUGE

4 groups of 3dc in pattern x 7.5 rows = 4 in. (10 cm) square

FINISHED SIZE

Circumference approx 17 in (43 cm)

To fit children 4–12 years old

INSTRUCTIONS

Using yarn A and the H-8 (5 mm) hook, ch91. Work the Crosshatch stitch (see page 86) for 17 rows.

Work in stripe pattern using the following colors: one row yarn A, one row yarn B, one row yarn C, one row yarn D, one row yarn E, repeat, ending with yarn B. Leaving a long tail, fasten off yarn. Thread yarn tail onto tapestry needle and weave it in through the last row made. Pull yarn gently to close the top of the hat and weave in the ends. Sew the side seam.

Attach yarn D to the bottom edge of the hat using the size 7 (4.5 mm) hook.

ROUND 1 Ch1, sc evenly around the edge of the hat, making approx 5 sts to each box of the crosshatch pattern. Join with a sl st to the first sc. Total approx 65 sts.

ROUND 2 Ch1, make 1sc in each st around; join with a sl st to the first sc.

ROUND 3 Ch1, make 1sc in each st around; join with sl st to the first sc. Fasten off the yarn and weave in the ends.

FINISHING

Make a pompom using a pompom maker or by cutting out two 3 in. (7.5 cm) disks of cardboard and cutting a 1 in. (2.5 cm) hole in the centers. Hold the two rings together and wind the remaining yarn C around them (passing it through the center) until the cardboard is completely covered. Cut through the wool around the outer edge of the disk, inserting the scirssors between the two pieces of cardboard. Cut a 12 in. (30 cm) length of yarn and tie it tightly around the center of the pompom. Remove the cardboard disks (you may need to cut them) and use your fingers to shape the pompom. Thread the ends of the yarn used to tie the pompom through the crown of the hat and stitch to secure.

Seed Stitch Stripe

A combination of chain and single crochet stitches create a dense, decorative fabric. Use up scraps of yarn by changing color every row, use a neutral background shade for every odd-numbered row and a series of contrasting brights for the even rows, or create solid stripes by changing color every three rows.

MATERIALS

Cascade Ultra Pima Fine (100% pima cotton; 1.75 oz/50 g; 136.5 yds /125 m) in colors of your choice

HOOK SIZE

G-6 (4 mm) crochet hook

SKILL LEVEL

Beginner

GAUGE

22sc in pattern x 22 rows = 4 in. (10 cm) square

FINISHED SIZE

4.75 x 5.25 in. (12 x 13 cm)

INSTRUCTIONS

Work a chain of a multiple of 2 sts plus 1, plus 3 sts for the Foundation Row.

FOUNDATION ROW Using yarn A, make 1sc in the 4th ch from the hook (counts as 1sc, ch1 and 1 skipped ch), *ch1, skip the next ch, make 1sc in the next ch; repeat from * to the end. Fasten off, turn.

ROW 1 Using yarn B, Ch2 (counts as 1sc, ch1), make 1sc in the first ch-1 sp, *ch1, make 1sc in the next ch-1 sp; repeat from * to the end, turn.

TO WORK THE PATTERN

Repeat Row 1, changing the color of the yarn as required.

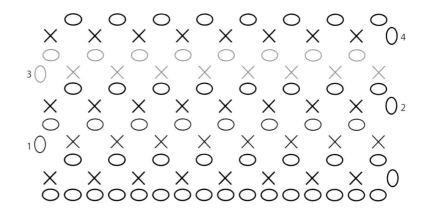

TRY THIS...

Use complementary colors to create an ombre stripe effect:

Magenta 3703 (yarn A)

Lipstick Red 3755 (yarn B)

Deep Coral 3767 (yarn C)

Tangerine 3750 (yarn D)

Buttercup 3748 (yarn E)

Natural 3718 (yarn F)

Textured Stripes

Single and treble crochet stitches combine to make an intriguing texture for this striped motif. Increase its visual appeal by using a combination of a neutral base color and complementary stripes, like those shown here, or add zing with contrasting stripes.

MATERIALS

Cascade Ultra Pima Fine
(100% pima cotton;
1.75 oz/50 g; 136.5 yds /125 m)

Taupe 3759 (yarn A)
Primrose 3712 (yarn B)
Cool Mint 3775 (yarn C)
Natural 3718 (yarn D)

HOOK SIZE

G-6 (4 mm) crochet hook

SKILL LEVEL

Intermediate

GAUGE

9 (1tr, 1sc) in pattern x 20 rows
= 4 in. (10 cm) square

FINISHED SIZE

4.75 x 5.5 in. (12 x 14 cm)

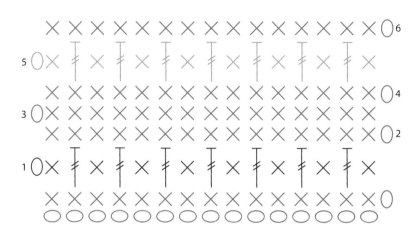

Tablet Cozy

Protect your tablet with a fitted crochet cover and make a smaller version for your cell phone.

MATERIALS

Scraps of Cascade Ultra Pima Fine (100% pima cotton; 1.75 oz/50 g; 136.5 yds /125 m), or a similar sportweight yarn

NOTIONS

Size E-4 (3.5 mm) crochet hook; adjust size to obtain correct gauge

GAUGE

9 (1tr, 1sc) in pattern x 20 rows = 4 in. (10 cm) square

FINISHED SIZE

9 x 6.5 in. (23 x 16.5 cm) to fit a 9.5 x 7.5 in. (24 x 19 cm) tablet

INSTRUCTIONS

Ch30, using the Textured Stripe Motif (see left), work 43 rows, finishing with Row 2. Do not fasten off. Ch1, make 1sc in the row end sts on the first side (43 sts); make 2sc in the corner, make 1sc in each st along the bottom (29 sts), make 2sc in the corner, make 1sc in each row end st on the 2nd side (43 sts), make 2sc in the corner, make 1sc along the top (29 sts), make 2sc in the corner. Join with a sl st to first sc made. Repeat to make a second piece.

FINISHING

Holding both pieces together, with WS facing, join the yarn in the top right-hand corner and ch1. Working into 2 loops of each piece (4 loops in total), work crab stitch in each st around on three sides. Sl st into the last sc. Fasten off. Work crab stitch along the 2 open sides. Fasten off. Weave in the ends.

INSTRUCTIONS

Work a chain of a multiple of 2 sts plus 1, plus 1 for the Foundation Row.

FOUNDATION ROW (RS) Using yarn A, make 1sc in the 2nd ch from the hook, and make 1sc in each ch to the end. Fasten off and change to yarn B, turn.

ROW 1 (WS) Ch1, make 1sc in the first st, * 1tr in the next st, make 1sc in the next st; repeat from * to the end of the row. Fasten off and change to yarn A, turn.

ROWS 2–4 Ch1, make 1sc in each st to the end of the row. Fasten off and change to yarn C, turn.

TO WORK THE PATTERN

Repeat Rows 1–4, changing the color at the end of the following rows:

Row 5: Change to yarn A.
Row 8: Change to yarn D.
Row 9: Change to yarn A.
Row 12: Change to yarn B.
Row 13: Change to yarn A.
Row 16: Change to yarn C.
Row 17: Change to yarn A.
Row 20: Change to yarn D.
Row 21: Change to yarn A.

Calming Waves

The rows of this striped motif combine stitches of different lengths to create elegant waves of color. By changing the shade every two rows you can create a graphic pattern of rhythmic interlocking stripes, which resemble waves on a calm sea.

MATERIALS

Cascade Ultra Pima Fine
(100% pima cotton; 1.75 oz/50 g;
136.5 yds /125 m)

Cool Mint 3775 (yarn A)
Spring Green 3762 (yarn B)
Ice 3736 (yarn C)
Teal 3734 (yarn D)
Natural 3718 (yarn E)
Chartreuse 3746 (yarn F)

HOOK SIZE

G-6 (4 mm) crochet hook

SKILL LEVEL

Intermediate

GAUGE

17sc in pattern x 15 rows = 4 in.
(10 cm) square

FINISHED SIZE

5.25 x 6.5 in. (13.5 x 16.5 cm)

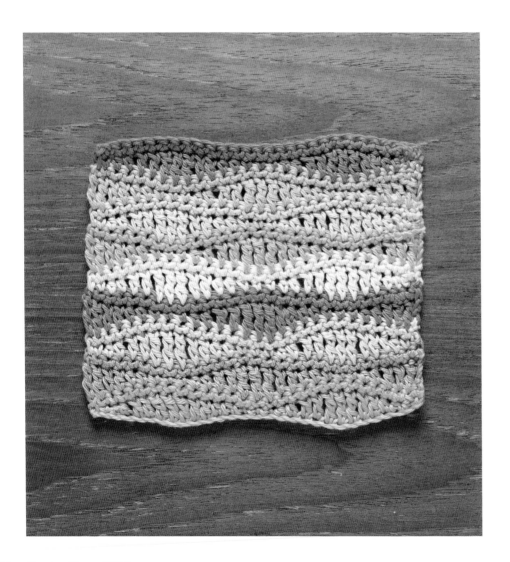

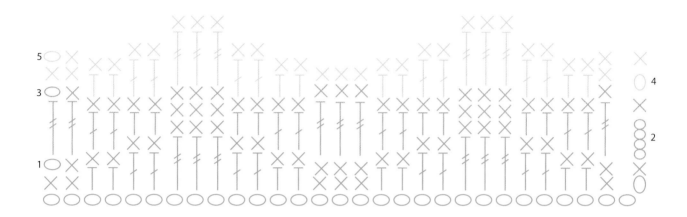

INSTRUCTIONS

Work a chain of a multiple of 14 sts plus 2 for the Foundation Row.

FOUNDATION ROW Using yarn A, make 1sc in the 3rd ch from hook (counts as 1ch and 1sc), * 1hdc in each of the next 2 ch, make 1dc in each of next the 2 ch, make 1tr in each of the next 3 ch, make 1dc in each of the next 2 ch, make 1hdc in each of the next 2 ch, make 1sc in each of the next 3 ch; repeat from * to ending with 1sc in each of last 2 ch, turn.

ROW 1 Ch1 (counts as 1sc), skip the first st, make 1sc in each st to the end of the row; make the last sc in t-ch. Fasten off yarn, turn.

ROW 2 Using yarn B, ch4 (counts as 1tr), skip the first st, * 1tr in the next st, make 1dc in each of the next 2 sts, make 1hdc in each of the next 2 sts, make 1sc in each of the next 3 sts, make 1hdc in each of the next 2 sts, make 1dc in each of the next 2 sts, make 1tr in each of the next 2 sts; repeat from *; make the last tr in the t-ch, turn.

ROW 3 Ch1 (counts as 1sc), skip the first st, make 1sc in each st to the end of the row; make the last sc in the t-ch. Fasten off, turn.

ROW 4 Using yarn C, ch1 (counts as 1sc). Skip the first sc, * 1sc in the next st, make 1hdc in each of the next 2 sts, make 1dc in each of the next 2 sts, make 1tr in each of the next 3 sts, make 1dc in each of the next 2 sts, make1hdc in each of the next 2 sts, make 1sc in each of the next 2 sts; repeat from * to end; make the last sc in the t-ch, turn.

TO WORK THE PATTERN

Repeat Rows 1–4, changing the yarn color after every two rows as follows:

Row 5: Yarn C.
Rows 6 and 7: Yarn D.
Rows 8 and 9: Yarn E.
Rows 10 and 11: Yarn A.
Rows 12 and 13: Yarn C.
Rows 14 and 15: Yarn F.
Rows 16 and 17: Yarn D.

Clusters and V-Stitch Stripe

Take your crochet to the next level with this combination of cluster and V-stitches worked in rows. Try using neutral-colored V-stitch rows to enhance a series of contrasting color cluster rows, or to set off a set of ombre shades.

MATERIALS

Cascade Ultra Pima Fine (100% pima cotton; 1.75 oz/50 g; 136.5 yds /125 m)

Natural 3718 (yarn A)
Taupe 3759 (yarn B)
Deep Coral 3767 (yarn C)
Teal 3734 (yarn D)
Cool Mint 3775 (yarn E)
Ice 3736 (yarn F)

HOOK SIZE

G-6 (4 mm) crochet hook

SKILL LEVEL

Intermediate

GAUGE

9 clusters x 10 rows = 4 in. (10 cm) square

FINISHED SIZE

5.5 x 4.25 in. (14 x 10.75 cm)

INSTRUCTIONS

Work a chain of a multiple of 2 sts plus 1, plus 2 sts for the Foundation Row.

FOUNDATION ROW Using yarn A, make 1hdc in the 3rd ch from the hook (counts as 2hdc), * skip 1 ch, (1hdc, ch1, 1hdc) in the next ch; repeat from * to the end. Fasten off and change to yarn B, turn.

ROW 1 Ch3 (counts as 1dc), make 1dc in the first st, ch1, *dc3tog in the next ch-1 sp, ch1; repeat from * ending with dc2tog in the top of the t-ch. Fasten off and change to yarn A, turn.

ROW 2 Ch2 (counts as 1hdc), * (1hdc, ch1, 1hdc) (V-st made) in the next ch-1 sp; repeat from * ending with 1hdc in the top of the t-ch. Fasten off and change to yarn C, turn.

ROW 3 Ch3 (counts as 1dc), *dc3tog in next ch-1 sp, ch1; repeat from * ending with 1dc in the top of the t-ch sp. Fasten off and change to yarn A, turn.

ROW 4 Ch2 (counts as 1hdc, make 1hdc in the same st, * (1hdc, 1ch, 1hdc) (V-st made) in the next ch-1 sp; repeat from * to the end. Fasten off and change to yarn D, turn.

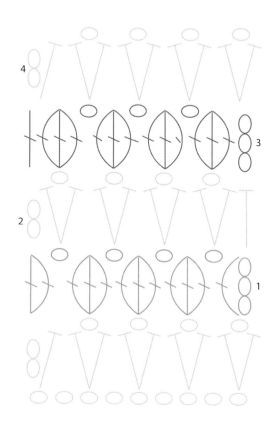

TO WORK THE PATTERN

Repeat Rows 1–4, working the stripes as follows: all V-st (hdc) rows (Rows 2 and 4) in yarn A and contrasting colors B, C, D, E, and F in (dc3tog) cluster rows (Rows 1 and 3).

V-Stitch Stripe

The V-stitch is a simple way to create an open-textured fabric versatile enough to be used for anything from blankets and scarves to sweaters. Our sample uses a series of complementary colors, but this stitch looks just as good in a single shade.

MATERIALS

Cascade Ultra Pima Fine (100% pima cotton; 1.75 oz/50 g; 136.5 yds /125 m)

Ice 3736 (yarn A)
Heathered Pansy 3705 (yarn B)
Coral 3752 (yarn C)
Natural 3718 (yarn D)
Cool Mint 3775 (yarn E)
Deep Coral 3767 (yarn F)
Gray 3729 (yarn G)

HOOK SIZE

G-6 (4 mm) crochet hook

SKILL LEVEL

Intermediate

GAUGE

7 V-st x 9 rows = 4 in. (10 cm) square

FINISHED SIZE

4.25 x 4.75 in. (10.5 x 12 cm)

INSTRUCTIONS

Work a chain of a multiple of 3 sts plus 2, plus 1 for the Foundation Row.

FOUNDATION ROW With yarn A (1dc, ch1, 1dc) (V-st made) in the 4th ch from the hook, * skip 2 chs, make V-st in the next ch; repeat from * to end, making 1dc in the last ch. Fasten off, turn.

ROW 1 Using yarn B, Ch3 (counts as 1dc), *V-st in the next ch-1 sp; repeat from * to end. Make 1dc in the t-ch sp. Fasten off, turn.

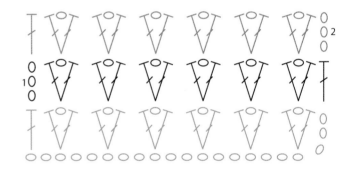

TO WORK THE PATTERN

Repeat Row 1, changing color at the end of each row as follows:

Row 2: Change to yarn C.
Row 3: Change to yarn D.
Row 4: Change to yarn E.
Row 5: Change to yarn F.
Row 6: Change to yarn A.

Row 7: Change to yarn D.
Row 8: Change to yarn C.
Row 9: Change to yarn G.

Lace Shell Stitch

Groups of double crochet stitches create pretty shells, which are separated by chain stitches to form a reversible, lace-like fabric, perfect for shawls and blankets. We have used a series of three colors to create the stripes of interlocking shells.

MATERIALS

Cascade Ultra Pima Fine (100% pima cotton; 1.75 oz/50 g; 136.5 yds / 125 m)

Spring Green 3762 (yarn A)
Primrose 3712 (yarn B)
Natural 3718 (yarn C)

HOOK SIZE

G-6 (4 mm) crochet hook

SKILL LEVEL

Intermediate

GAUGE

2 shells x 12 rows = 4 in. (10 cm) square

FINISHED SIZE

5 x 7.5 in. (12.5 x 19 cm) long

INSTRUCTIONS

Work a chain of a multiple of 8 sts plus 4 for the Foundation Row.

FOUNDATION ROW Using yarn A, make 2dc in the 4th ch from the hook, (half shell made) * ch2, skip the next 3 chs. Make 1sc in the next ch, ch2, skip the next 3 chs, make 5dc (shell) in the next ch; repeat from *, ending with 3dc (half shell) in the last ch. Fasten off and change to yarn B, turn.

ROW 1 Ch1, sc in the first st, * ch2, make 5dc in the sc, ch2, make 1sc in center dc of the shell; repeat from *, ending with 1sc on the top of the t-ch. Fasten off and change to yarn C, turn.

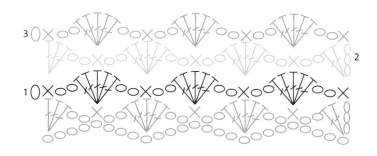

ROW 2 Ch3 (counts as first dc), make 2dc in the same st, * ch2, make 1sc in the center dc of the shell, ch2, make 5dc in the sc; repeat from *, ending with 3dc in the last sc. Fasten off and change to yarn A, turn.

TO WORK THE PATTERN Repeat Rows 1 and 2, changing color at the end of every row as follows: one row yarn A, one row yarn B, one row yarn C.

MATERIALS

Cascade Ultra Pima Fine
(100% pima cotton; 1.75 oz/50 g;
136.5 yds /125 m), or a similar
sportweight yarn

Pink Rose 3776 (yarn A) x 2 balls
Chartreuse 3746 (yarn B) x 2 balls
Blood Orange 3804 (yarn C) x 2 balls
Sand 3717 (yarn D) x 2 balls
Gold 3747 (yarn E) x 2 balls

NOTIONS

Size 7 (4.5 mm) crochet hook;
adjust size if necessary to obtain
correct gauge

Darning needle

GAUGE

2 shells x 12 rows = 4 in.
(10 cm) square

FINISHED SIZE

33 x 28 in. (84 x 71 cm)

Lace Shell Baby Blanket

A homemade gift, stitched with love, is satisfying to give and to receive
and will become a treasured heirloom. For a modern color scheme,
combine bright, citrus hues with light and airy lace shell stitch stripes.
The ideal size for a crib or stroller, choose a machine-wash cotton yarn
to make it as easy to care for as it is a pleasure to use.

INSTRUCTIONS

Using yarn A, ch100.
Complete 75 rows using the Lace Shell
Stitch (see page 99) using yarns in the
following order:
Row 1: Yarn A.
Row 2: Yarn B.
Row 3: Yarn C.
Row 4: Yarn D.
Row 5: Yarn E.
Repeat Rows 1–5 15 times.

EDGING

ROUND 1 Using yarn C, work the first
round of the border as follows:

TOP Start the border in the top right-hand
corner. Ch1, (1sc, ch2, 1sc) in the same st.
Make 1sc in each of the next 2 sts, * 1hdc
in the bottom, 1dc in the sc, 1hdc in the
ch-2 sp, 1sc in the next 5 sts; repeat fromn
* to the last 3 sts. Make 1sc in the next 2
sts, and (1sc, ch2, 1sc) in the corner.

SIDE 1 * 2sc in each shell, make 1sc in
each sc; repeat from * along the side of the
blanket to the end, and work (1sc, ch2,
1sc) in the corner.

BOTTOM * 3sc in the first ch loop, make 1sc
in the next st, 3sc in the ch loop, 1sc in the
bottom of the 5dc; repeat from * to the end
of the row, and work (1sc, ch2, 1sc) in the
corner.

SIDE 2 * 2sc in each shell, make 1sc in
each sc; repeat from * along the side of the
blanket, ending with a sl st in the first sc
made. Fasten off.

ROUND 2 Using yarn D, join with a sl st to
any st from the previous row. Work 1sc in
each st around, and make (1sc, ch2, 1sc)
in each corner. Fasten off.

ROUND 3 Using yarn E, join with a sl st to
any st from the previous row. Work 1hdc in
each st around and make (1hdc, ch2, 1hdc)
in each corner. Fasten off.

Solid Shell Stitch

This dense, textured fabric uses groups of double crochet stitches to create a series of fan-like shells, which provide plenty of visual interest. Our sample uses just two contrasting colors, but this stitch makes an ideal setting for multicolored stripes.

MATERIALS

Cascade Ultra Pima Fine (100% pima cotton; 1.75 oz/50 g; 136.5 yds /125 m)

Turquoise 3733 (yarn A)
Gray 3729 (yarn B)

HOOK SIZE

G-6 (4 mm) crochet hook

SKILL LEVEL

Intermediate

GAUGE

3 shells x 11 rows = 4 in. (10 cm) square

FINISHED SIZE

5.5 x 6.5 in. (14 x 16.5 cm)

INSTRUCTIONS

Work a chain of a multiple of 6 sts, plus 2 for the Foundation Row.

FOUNDATION ROW (RS) Using yarn A, make 1sc in 2nd ch from the hook, * skip the next 2 ch, make 5dc in the next ch (shell made), skip the next 2 ch, make 1sc in the next ch; repeat from *, ending with 1sc in the last ch. Finish off and change to yarn B, turn.

ROW 1 Ch3 (counts as first dc), make 2dc in the first st, * skip the next 2 sts, make 1sc in the next st (center dc of the shell), skip the next 2 sts, make 5dc in the next st (sc from previous row); repeat from *, ending with 3dc in the last st. Finish off and change to yarn A, turn.

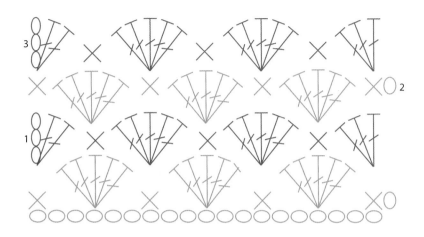

ROW 2 Ch1, make 1sc in the first st, * skip the next 2 sts, make 5dc in the next st, skip the next 2 sts, make 1sc in the next st; repeat from *, ending with 1sc on the top of the t-ch. Finish off and change to yarn B, turn.

TO WORK THE PATTERN
Repeat Rows 1 and 2 a total of 7 times. Fasten off.

TRY THIS...
Play with contrasting colors to create eye-catching stripes:
Pansy 3779 (yarn A)
Cool Mint 3775 (yarn B)
Sand 3717 (yarn C)

Zigzags

Crochet ripples build up to form a calming sea of color and these simple repeated stitch patterns will help you to unwind as you make them. Use these zigzag stripes as the basis for a chunky rug, elegant lace scarf, or a spacious tote bag.

RUG

Use a super chunky yarn to make a thick rug for a bedroom or bathroom floor, or even as a liner for a dog's bed. Choose colors that complement your decor—or use them to create an eye-catching contrast. For the instructions to make this design, see page 107.

Single Crochet Zigzags

Rows of single crochet stitches worked in zigzags create a solid fabric with plenty of texture. Increase the visual interest by changing the yarn color every two rows. Create bold stripes by changing color every two rows, or create a color explosion by changing every row.

MATERIALS

Cascade Ultra Pima Fine
(100% pima cotton; 1.75 oz/50 g;
136.5 yds /125 m)

Gray 3729 (yarn A)
Natural 3718 (yarn B)
Cool Mint 3775 (yarn C)
Ice 3736 (yarn D)
Coral 3752 (yarn E)
Taupe 3759 (yarn F)

HOOK SIZE

G-6 (4 mm) crochet hook

SKILL LEVEL

Beginner

GAUGE

24sc x 9 rows = 4 in.
(10 cm) square

FINISHED SIZE

5 x 5.5 in. (13 x 14cm)

Rug

A warm rug is just the thing to step on when you get up on a chilly morning.

MATERIALS

Tivoli Maxi (80% acrylic, 20% wool; 3.5 oz/100g; 109 yds/100 m) in colors A–D. 2 balls each of Gray 837 (yarn A), Cerise 841 (yarn B), Green 832 (yarn C), Natural 830 (yarn D), or a similar super chunky weight yarn.

NOTIONS

Size M/N-13 (9 mm) crochet hook; adjust size to obtain correct gauge

GAUGE

1 zigzag x 12 rows = 4 in. (10 cm) square

FINISHED SIZE

30 x 38 in. (76 x 96.5 cm)

INSTRUCTIONS

Using yarn A, ch79. Work 132 rows of single crochet zigzag (see left) in the following color sequence—2 rows yarn A, 2 rows yarn B, 2 rows yarn C, 2 rows yarn D, and finish with 2 rows of yarn A.

FINISHING

ROW 1 Using yarn A, join in one corner st, ready to work along one side of the rug. Ch1, make 1sc in the side of each st of the row to the next corner, turn.

ROW 2 Ch1, skip the first st. Make 1sc in each st to the end of the row; join with a sl st in the corner st. Fasten off.

Repeat Rows 1 and 2 for the other side of the rug. Weave in the ends and block if necessary.

INSTRUCTIONS

Work a chain of a multiple of 11 sts, plus 2 for the Foundation Row.

FOUNDATION ROW Using yarn A, make 2sc in the 2nd ch from the hook, make 1sc in each of the next 4 chs, skip the next 2 ch, make 1sc in each of the next 4 ch, * 3sc in the next ch, make 1sc in each of the next 4 ch, skip 2 ch, make 1sc in each of the next 4 ch; repeat from * to last ch, make 2sc in the last ch, turn.

ROW 1 Ch1 and make 2sc in the first st, * 1sc in each of the next 4 sts, skip the next 2 sts, make 1sc in each of the next 4 sts, make 3sc in the next st; repeat from * and end with 2sc in the last st, turn.

TO WORK THE PATTERN

Repeat Row 1 for the pattern, changing the yarn color after every two rows as follows:

Foundation Row and Row 1: Yarn A.
Rows 2 and 3: Yarn B.
Rows 4 and 5: Yarn C.
Rows 6 and 7: Yarn D.
Rows 8 and 9: Yarn A.
Rows 10 and 11: Yarn E.
Rows 12 and 13: Yarn B.
Rows 14 and 15: Yarn F.
Rows 16 and 17: Yarn C.
Rows 18 and 19: Yarn E.
Rows 20 and 21: Yarn A.

Gentle Ripple Zigzags

Undulating waves of double crochet stitches build rows of color. Groups of three double crochet stitches worked together shape the rows into ripples. Experiment with color combinations, using bright and natural shades for the ultimate in contrasts.

MATERIALS

Cascade Ultra Pima Fine (100% pima cotton; 1.75 oz/50 g; 136.5 yds /125 m)

Magenta 3703 (yarn A)
Buff 3719 (yarn B)
Primrose 3712 (yarn C)
Tangerine 3750 (yarn D)
Chocolate 3716 (yarn E)
Sand 3717 (yarn F)
Lipstick Red 3755 (yarn G)
Natural 3718 (yarn H)
Coral 3752 (yarn I)

HOOK SIZE

G-6 (4 mm) crochet hook

SKILL LEVEL

Intermediate

GAUGE

22dc in pattern x 6 rows = 4 in. (10 cm) square

FINISHED SIZE

6.5 x 4.5 in. (16.5 x 11.5 cm)

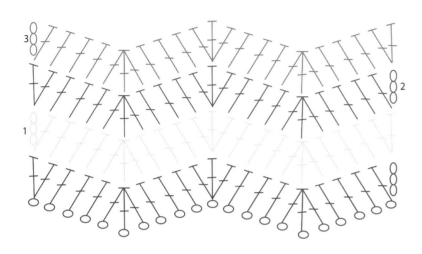

INSTRUCTIONS

Work a chain of a multiple of 10 sts plus 1, plus 3 for the Foundation Row.

FOUNDATION ROW Using yarn A, make 1dc in the 4th ch from the hook (counts as 2dc), * 1dc in each of the next 3 ch, dc3tog over the next 3 ch, make 1dc in each of the next 3 ch, make 3dc in the next ch; repeat from *, ending the last repeat with 2dc in the last ch. Fasten off and change to yarn B, turn.

ROW 1 Ch3, make 1dc in the first st (counts as 2dc), * 1dc in each of the next 3 sts, dc3tog over the next 3 sts, make 1dc in each of the next 3 sts, make 3dc in the next st; repeat from *, ending the last repeat with 2dc in the t-ch. Fasten off, change to yarn C, and turn.

TO WORK THE PATTERN

Repeat Row 1 for the pattern, changing the yarn color after every row as follows:

Row 2: Yarn C.
Row 3: Yarn D.
Row 4: Yarn E.
Row 5: Yarn F.
Row 6: Yarn G.
Row 7: Yarn H.
Row 8: Yarn I.
Row 9: Yarn E.

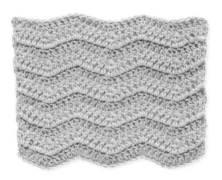

TRY THIS...

Playing with color contrasts enables these bright yellow stripes to appear to explode from a pale green background:

Sage 3720 (yarn A)
Sunshine 3764 (yarn B)

Granny Ripple Zigzags

There's a pleasing rhythm working patterns based on the Granny Square. Here, the motif's group of double crochet stitches are arranged in zigzags that suit a selection of ombre shades. The ombre assortment of colors is highlighted by a zing of citrus color.

MATERIALS

Cascade Ultra Pima Fine
(100% pima cotton; 1.75 oz/50 g;
136.5 yds /125 m)

Jade 3735 (yarn A)
Cool Mint 3775 (yarn B)
Ice 3736 (yarn C)
Chartreuse 3746 (yarn D)

HOOK SIZE

G-6 (4 mm) crochet hook

SKILL LEVEL

Beginner

GAUGE

8 3dc clusters worked in pattern x 8 rows = 4 in. (10 cm) square

FINISHED SIZE

7 x 4.5 in. (17.75 x 11.5 cm)

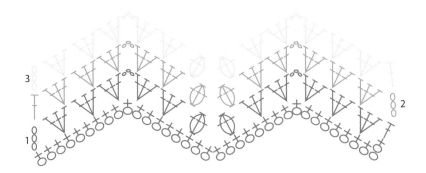

INSTRUCTIONS

Work a chain of a multiple of 17 sts plus 1, plus 1 for the Foundation Row.

FOUNDATION ROW Using yarn A, make 1sc into the 2nd chain from the hook and make 1sc into each ch until the end of row, turn.

ROW 1 Using yarn A, ch3 (counts as 1dc), skip the first 3 sts, (3dc in the next st, skip the next 2 sts) twice, (3dc, ch3, 3dc) in the next st, * skip the next 2 sts, make 3dc in the next st, skip the next 2 sts, dc3tog in the next st, skip the next 4 sts, dc3tog in the next st, skip the next 2 sts, make 3dc in the next st, skip the next 2 sts, (3dc, ch3, 3dc) in the next st; repeat from * to the last 8 sts, skip the next 2 sts, 3dc in the next st, skip the next 2 sts, 3dc in the next st, skip the next st, make 1dc in the last st. Fasten off and change to yarn B, turn.

ROW 2 Ch3 (counts as 1dc), skip the first 4dc, make 3dc into each of the next 2 sps, (3dc, ch3, 3dc) in next ch-3 sp, * 3dc in the next sp, dc3tog in the next space, skip the next sp (bet dc3tog cls), dc3tog in the next space, make 3dc in the next space, (3dc, ch3, 3dc) in the next 3-ch sp; repeat from * to last 3 sps, make 3dc in each of the next 2 sps, make 1dc in the t-ch. Fasten off and change yarn, turn.

TO WORK THE PATTERN

Repeat Row 2 and work in the color sequence as follows:
Row 3: Yarn C.
Row 4: Yarn D.
Row 5: Yarn A.
Row 6: Yarn B.
Row 7: Yarn C.
Row 8: Yarn D.
Row 9: Yarn A.

TRY THIS...

Toning pastels create gentle waves of color when used to create stripes:
Ice 3736 (yarn A)
Coral 3752 (yarn B)
Sand 3717 (yarn C)
Yellow Rose 3743 (yarn D)

Eyelet Ripple Zigzags

To create semisolid rows of stitches, use chain stitches to create eyelets between groups of double crochet stitches. Ombre colors, combined with a contrasting bright shade, add visual interest. This easy-to-remember pattern works up quickly for throws and blankets.

MATERIALS

Cascade Ultra Pima Fine
(100% pima cotton; 1.75 oz/50 g;
136.5 yds / 125 m)

Delphinium 3706 (yarn A)
Pansy 3779 (yarn B)
Wood Violet 3709 (yarn C)
Cool Mint 3775 (yarn D)

HOOK SIZE

G-6 (4 mm) crochet hook

SKILL LEVEL

Intermediate

GAUGE

18dc worked in pattern x 9 rows
= 4 in. (10 cm) square

FINISHED SIZE

5.75 x 4.5 in. (14.5 x 11.5 cm)

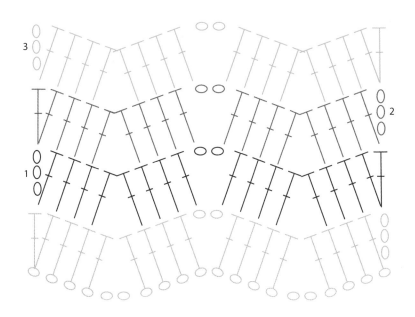

INSTRUCTIONS

Work a chain of a multiple of 10 sts, plus 3 for the Foundation Row.

FOUNDATION ROW Using yarn A, make 1dc into the 4th ch from the hook (counts as 2dc), make 1dc in the next 3 ch, skip 2ch, make 1dc in the next 4 ch, ch2, * make 1dc in the next 4 ch, skip 2chs, make 1dc in the next 4ch, ch2; repeat from * to the last 6ch, skip 2 ch, make 1dc in the next 3ch, make 2dc in the last ch, fasten off, and change to yarn B, turn.

ROW 1 Ch3 (counts as 1dc), make 1dc in the same st, make 1dc in the next 3 sts, * skip 2 sts, make 1dc in the next 3 sts, (1dc, ch2, 1dc) in the next ch-2 sp, make 1dc in the next 3 sts; repeat from * to the last 6 sts, skip 2 sts, make 1dc in the next 3 sts, make 2dc in the t-ch, fasten off, and change to yarn C, turn.

TO WORK THE PATTERN

Repeat Row 1 and work in the color sequence as follows:
Row 2: Yarn C.
Row 3: Yarn D.
Row 4: Yarn A.
Row 5: Yarn B.
Row 6: Yarn C.
Row 7: Yarn D.
Row 8: Yarn A.
Row 9: Yarn B.

MATERIALS

Cascade Pacific (60% acrylic and 40% Merino wool; 3.5 oz/ 100 g; 213 yds/195 m); or a similar worsted weight yarn

Beet 53 (yarn A) x 1 ball
Honeysuckle Pink 51 (yarn B) x 1 ball
Peacock 40 (yarn C) x 1 ball
Grass 86 (yarn D) x 1 ball
Dusty Turquoise 23 (yarn E) x 1 ball
Cream 01 (yarn F) x 1 ball
Almond 60 (yarn G) x 1 ball

NOTIONS

Size 7 (4.5 mm) crochet hook; adjust size if necessary to obtain correct gauge

Darning needle

GAUGE

10dc worked in pattern x 8 rows = 4 in. (10 cm) square

FINISHED SIZE

72 x 9.5 in. (183 x 24 cm)

PROJECT

Eyelet Ripple Zigzags Scarf

This simple lace stitch is satisfying to work as it quickly builds up to make a scarf. The bright colors used here will boost your spirits on a chilly winter's day. The scarf is long enough to wrap around your neck a couple of times. For a shorter scarf, use a shorter foundation chain– just make sure it is in a multiple of 10 stitches, plus 3.

INSTRUCTIONS

Using yarn A, ch283 sts and work the Foundation Row of the Eyelet Ripple Zigzags motif (see page 112), fasten off, join yarn B, turn, and work Row 1

ROWS 2–16 Repeat Row 1 for the pattern and work in the color sequence as follows:
ROW 2: Yarn B.
ROW 3: Yarn C.
ROW 4: Yarn D.
ROW 5: Yarn E.
ROW 6: Yarn F.
ROW 7: Yarn B.
ROW 8: Yarn G.
ROW 9: Yarn A.
ROW 10: Yarn C.
ROW 11: Yarn E.
ROW 12: Yarn G.
ROW 13: Yarn F.
ROW 14: Yarn D.
ROW 15: Yarn B.
ROW 16: Yarn A. Do not fasten off yarn A.

EDGING

Ch1, make 1sc in each st and make 2sc in each ch-2 sp to the end of the row. Continue around, making 2sc in each corner, and make 2sc into the side of each end of row st along both sides of the scarf, and 1sc in each ch of the foundation ch along the bottom of the scarf. Join with a sl st to the first sc made.

FINISHING

Weave in all ends and lightly steam block the scarf into shape.

Deep Ripple Zigzags

Striped single rows of double crochet quickly work up to create fabric with a dramatic zigzag pattern. Use it to try out new color combinations, including summery ice-cream shades separated by rows of a neutral shade (perfect for a picnic blanket)!

MATERIALS

Cascade Ultra Pima Fine (100% pima cotton; 1.75 oz/50 g; 136.5 yds /125 m)

Natural 3718 (MC)
Buttercup 3748 (yarn A)
Spring Green 3762 (yarn B)
Tangerine 3750 (yarn C)
Cool Mint 3775 (yarn D)

HOOK SIZE

G-6 (4 mm) crochet hook

SKILL LEVEL

Beginner

GAUGE

26dc worked in pattern x 8 rows = 4 in. (10 cm) square

FINISHED SIZE

5.5 x 5 in. (14 x 12.5cm)

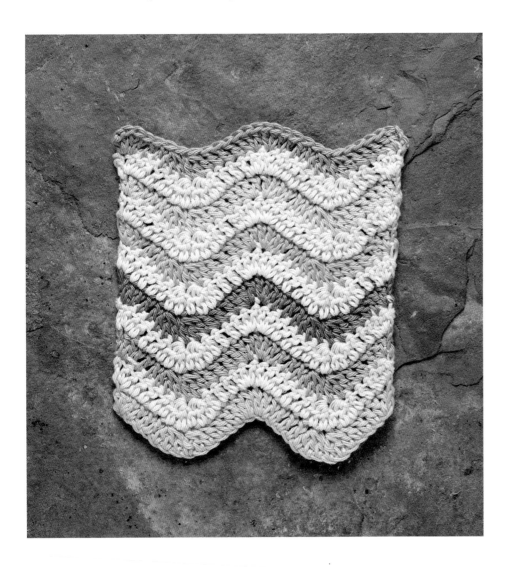

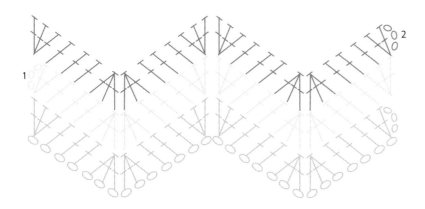

INSTRUCTIONS

Work a chain of a multiple of 14 sts, plus 3 for the Foundation Row.

FOUNDATION ROW Using yarn A, make 2dc in the 4th ch from the hook (counts as 3dc), make 1dc in each of the next 3ch, (dc3tog over the next 3ch) twice, * 1dc in each of the next 3 ch, (3dc in the next ch) twice, make 1dc in each of the next 3 ch, (dc3tog over the next 3 ch) twice; repeat from * to last 4 ch; make 1dc in each of the next 3 ch, make 3dc in the last ch. Fasten off and change to MC, turn.

ROW 1 Ch3 (counts as 1dc) and make 2dc in first st; * 1dc in each of the next 3 sts, (dc3tog over the next 3 sts) twice, make 1dc in each of the next 3 sts, (3dc in the next st) twice; repeat from * ending with 3dc in the t-ch. Fasten off and change to yarn B, turn.

TO WORK THE PATTERN

Repeat Row 1 and work in the color sequence as follows:
Row 2: Yarn B.
Row 3: Yarn MC.
Row 4: Yarn C.
Row 5: Yarn MC.
Row 6: Yarn D.
Row 7: Yarn MC.
Row 8: Yarn A.
Row 9: Yarn MC.
Row 10: Yarn B.

TRY THIS...

Bright greens and pinks stand out against rows of neutral stitches:
Sand 3717 (yarn A)
Chartreuse 3746 (yarn B)
Dark Sea Foam 3797 (yarn C)
Primrose 3712 (yarn D)

Feather Stitch Zigzags

This pretty stitch is perfect for afghans and blankets, especially when combined with a selection of vintage-inspired colors. The clusters of double crochet stitches framed by eyelets create a surprisingly substantial fabric with plenty of visual interest.

MATERIALS

Cascade Ultra Pima Fine
(100% pima cotton; 1.75 oz/50 g;
136.5 yds /125 m)

Spring Green 3762 (yarn A)
Coral 3752 (yarn B)
Sand 3717 (yarn C)
Yellow Rose 3743 (yarn D)
Deep Coral 3767 (yarn E)

HOOK SIZE

G-6 (4 mm) crochet hook

SKILL LEVEL

Intermediate

GAUGE

6 clusters x 5.5 rows = 4 in. (10 cm) square

FINISHED SIZE

5.5 x 4.75 in. (14 x 12cm)

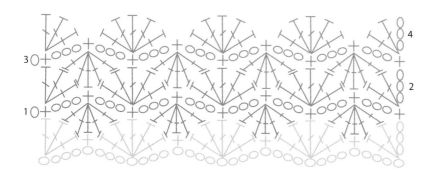

INSTRUCTIONS

Work a chain of a multiple of 8 sts, plus 4 for the Foundation Row.

FOUNDATION ROW Using yarn A, make 2dc in the 4th ch from the hook (counts as 3dc), skip the next 3 ch, make 1sc in the next ch, * skip the next 3 ch, make 5dc in the next ch, skip the next 3 chs, make 1sc in the next ch; repeat from * to the last 4 ch, skip the next 3 ch, make 3dc in the last ch. Fasten off and change to yarn B.

ROW 1 Ch1, make 1sc in the first st, * ch3, dc5tog over the next 5 sts, ch3, make 1sc in the next st; repeat from *, ending with the last sc in the t-ch.

ROW 2 Ch3 (counts as 1dc) and make 2dc in the first st, skip the ch-3 sp, * 1sc in the next st (top of dc5tog), skip the ch-3 sp, make 5dc in the next st, skip the ch-3 sp; repeat from * to the last ch-3 sp, make 3dc in the last st. Fasten off and change to yarn C.

TO WORK THE PATTERN

Repeat Rows 1 and 2 and work in the color sequence as follows:
Rows 3 and 4: Yarn C.
Row 5 and 6: Yarn D.
Rows 7 and 8: Yarn E.
Row 9 and 10: Yarn A.
Rows 11 and 12: Yarn B.

TRY THIS...

Jade contrasts with toning shades of purple to create bright stripes of color:
Wood Violet 3709 (yarn A)
Jade 3735 (yarn B)
Pansy 3779 (yarn C)

Thick and Thin Ripple Zigzags

Single and double crochet stitches create alternating narrow and deep rows of color that are perfect for using up leftover scraps of yarn from other projects. The result is a pattern that's easy to memorize and that creates a dense, textured fabric, which drapes well.

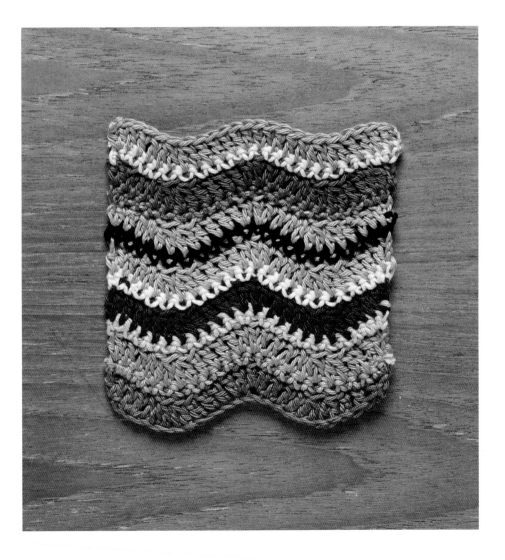

MATERIALS

Cascade Ultra Pima Fine
(100% pima cotton; 1.75 oz/50 g; 136.5 yds / 125 m)

Deep Coral 3767 (yarn A)
Sand 3717 (yarn B)
Teal 3734 (yarn C)
Yellow Rose 3743 (yarn D)
Magenta 3703 (yarn E)
Natural 3718 (yarn F)
Coral 3752 (yarn G)
True Black 3754 (yarn H)
Dark Sea Foam 3797 (yarn I)

HOOK SIZE

G-6 (4 mm) crochet hook

SKILL LEVEL

Intermediate

GAUGE

22dc in pattern x 11 rows = 4 in. (10 cm) square

FINISHED SIZE

5 x 4.75 in. (12.75 x 12 cm)

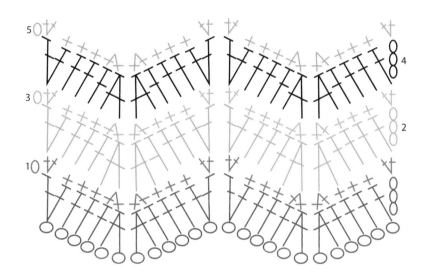

INSTRUCTIONS

Work a chain of a multiple of 12 sts, plus 3 for the Foundation Row.

FOUNDATION ROW Using yarn A, make 1dc in the 4th ch from the hook (2dc), make 1dc in each of the next 3 ch, (dc2tog over the next 2 ch) twice, make 1dc in each of the next 3 ch, (2dc in the next ch) twice, * 1dc in each of the next 3 ch, (dc2tog over the next 2 ch) twice, make 1dc in each of the next 3 ch, (2dc in the next ch) twice, repeat from * to the last ch, make 2dc in the last ch. Fasten off and change to yarn B, turn.

ROW 1 Ch1, make 2sc in the first st, make 1sc in each of the next 3 sts, (sc2tog over the next 2 sts) twice, make 1sc in each of the next 3 sts, * (2sc in the next st) twice, make 1sc in each of the next 3 sts, (sc2tog over the next 2 sts) twice, make 1sc in each of the next 3 sts; repeat from *, ending with 2sc in the t-ch. Fasten off and change to yarn C.

ROW 2 Ch3, make 1dc in the first st (2dc), * 1dc in each of the next 3 sts, (dc2tog over the next 2 sts) twice, make 1dc in each of the next 3 sts, (2dc in the next st) twice; repeat from * to the last st, make 2dc in the last st. Fasten off and change to yarn D, turn.

TO WORK THE PATTERN

Repeat Rows 1 and 2 and work in the color sequence as follows:
Row 3: Yarn D.
Row 4: Yarn E.
Row 5: Yarn F.
Row 6: Yarn G.
Row 7: Yarn H.
Row 8: Yarn B.
Row 9: Yarn A.
Row 10: Yarn I.
Row 11: Yarn D.
Row 12: Yarn C.

MATERIALS

Sirdar Cotton DK (100% cotton; 3.5 oz./100g; 232 yd./212 m) or a similar DK yarn

Pomegranate 530 (yarn A) x 2 balls
Bluebird 515 (yarn B) x 1 ball
Vanilla 502 (yarn C) x 1 ball
Toasted 505 (yarn D) x 1 ball
Light Taupe 504 (yarn E) x 1 ball
Tranquil 516 (yarn F) x 1 ball
Sundance 507 (yarn G) x 1 ball

2 pieces heavier weight lining fabric measuring 14.5 x. 14.5 in. (36.5 x 36.5 cm)

NOTIONS

Size E-4 (3.5 mm) crochet hook; adjust size if necessary to obtain correct gauge

Yarn and sewing needles

Pair of leather bag handles (see Notes, below)

Strong sewing thread

GAUGE

22dc in pattern x 11 rows = 4 in. (10 cm) square

FINISHED SIZE

14 x 14 x 2.5 in. (35.5 x 35.5 x 6.5 cm)

NOTES

Choose a pair of leather bag handles with ready-made stitching holes. Otherwise, you may struggle to push a needle through the leather.

PROJECT

Tote Bag

Bright colors are fun to work with and are guaranteed to lift your mood. This bag is perfect for any occasion—whether it's a trip to the market or a day at the beach. It is made from three pieces—front, back, and a long piece for the sides and base, and then it's sewn together. The finishing touches are a fabric lining and ready-made handles.

INSTRUCTIONS

The body of the bag is made using the Thick and Thin Ripple Zigzag pattern (see page 120). Row 1 and Row 37 of the pattern form a straight edge.

BAG BODY (MAKE 2)

The color sequence pattern is as follows: one row of yarn B, one row of yarn C, one row of yarn D, one row of yarn E, one row of yarn F, one row of yarn A, and one row of yarn G. Repeat for the body of the bag. Using yarn B, ch64.

FOUNDATION ROW Make 1tr in the 5th ch from the hook, make 1dc in each of he next 2 chs, make 1hdc in the next ch, make 1sc in each of the next 2 chs, make 1hdc in the next ch, make 1dc in each of the next 2 chs, make 2tr in the next ch, * 2tr in the next ch, make 1dc in each of the next 2 chs, make 1hdc in the next ch, make 1sc in each of the next 2 chs, make 1hdc in the next ch, make 1dc in each of the next 2 chs, make 2tr in the next ch; repeat from * to the end. Fasten off and change color. (72 sts) Starting with Row 2 of the Thick and Thin Ripple Zigzag pattern, repeat Rows 1 and 2 until 36 rows are made, finishing with Row 1 and yarn C. Fasten off.

ROW 37 Using yarn D, ch1. Make 1sc in the same st, make 1hdc in the next st, make 1dc in the next 2 sts, (tr2tog over the next 2 sts) twice, make 1dc in the next 2 sts, make 1hdc in the next st, make 1sc in the next st, * 1sc in the next st, make 1hdc in the next st, make 1dc in the next 2 sts, (tr2tog over the next 2 sts) twice, make 1dc in the next 2 sts, make 1hdc in the next st, make 1sc in the next st; repeat from * to the end. Fasten off and turn. (60 sts)

ROW 38 Join in yarn A and ch1. Make 1sc in each st across to the end, turn.

ROWS 39–49 Repeat Row 38. (12 rows) Mark Row 6 with a pin where the top will be folded over.

BAG SIDES AND BASE

Using yarn A, ch13.

ROW 1 Make 1sc in the 2nd ch from the hook, and make 1sc in each ch to the end, turn. (12sc)

ROWS 2–204 Ch1 and make 1sc in each st to the end, turn. Fasten off.

FINISHING

To line the bag, place the right sides of the two pieces of lining fabric together, and sew using a 0.25 in. (5 mm) seam allowance around three sides, leaving the top open. Press the seams open, fold the top edge down 0.25 in. (5 mm), press flat. Turn inside out, so that you can see the right side.

With the wrong sides of the crochet sections together, align the top of the long side panel at Row 6 on each side of the front panel, to allow the top piece to fold over. Continue pinning down one edge of the long side panel to the sides and lower edge of the front panel to ensure it is evenly distributed. Working through both thicknesses, join yarn A in the top left-hand corner of the front. Ch1 and sc evenly down the side of the front, across the lower edge, and up the next side. Fasten off. Repeat to join the back panel of the bag to the side panel.

Turn the crocheted bag inside out and slide the lining inside. Position the lining over the bag, pinning in place at the top edge, with the pressed 0.25 in. (5 mm) seam allowance folded under. You should

match the sewn seams with the halfway point of each edge of the long side panel to ensure that the lining is evenly dispersed around the bag. Be sure to pin the lining fabric edge along Row 6 of the front and back panels.

Using matching thread, blind-stitch the top edge of the lining fabric around the entire bag. Next, sew the two flaps to the lining, being careful not to stitch into the front and back panels. Position the handles, and using strong sewing thread, stitch through the lining fabric and crocheted piece in the premade handle holes.

Lace Ripple Zigzags

Delicate rows of double crochet and chain zigzags form a lace fabric enhanced by clusters of five stitches. Create a simple border by using contrasting colors for the first and last two rows and work the stitches in a single color for the rest of the fabric.

MATERIALS

Cascade Ultra Pima Fine (100% pima cotton; 1.75 oz/50 g; 136.5 yds / 125 m)

Taupe 3759 (yarn A)
Ice 3736 (yarn B)
Natural 3718 (yarn C)

HOOK SIZE

G-6 (4 mm) crochet hook

SKILL LEVEL

Intermediate

GAUGE

16dc worked in pattern x 6 rows = 4 in. (10 cm) square

FINISHED SIZE

6.5 x 5 in. (16.5 x 12.5cm)

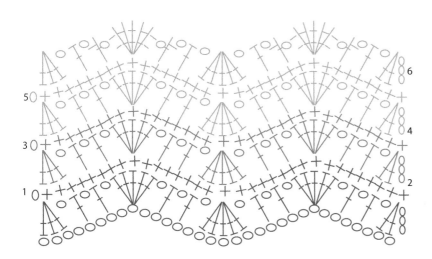

INSTRUCTIONS

Work a chain of a multiple of 16 sts, plus 3 for the Foundation Row.

FOUNDATION ROW Using yarn A, dc2tog over the 4th and 5th chs from the hook (counts as dc3tog), ch1, skip the next ch, (1dc in the next ch, ch1, skip the next ch) twice, make 5dc in the next ch, * ch1, skip the next ch, (1dc in the next ch, ch1, skip the next ch) twice, dc5tog over the next 5 ch, ch1, skip the next ch, (1dc in the next ch, ch1, skip the next ch) twice, make 5dc in the next ch; repeat from * to the last 8 ch, ch1, skip the next ch, (1dc in the next ch, ch1, skip the next ch) twice, dc3tog over the last 3ch, turn.

ROW 1 Ch1, make 1sc in each st and in every ch-1 sp to the end. Fasten off and change to yarn B, turn.

ROW 2 Using yarn B, ch3, skip the first st, dc2tog over the next 2 sts (counts as dc3tog), ch1, skip the next st, (1dc in the next st, ch1, skip the next st) twice, 5dc in the next st, * ch1, skip the next st, (1dc in the next st, ch1, skip the next st) twice, dc5tog over the next 5 sts, ch1, skip the next st, (make 1dc in the next st, ch1, skip the next st) twice, make 5dc in the next st; repeat from * to the last 8 sts, ch1, skip the next st, (1dc in the next st, ch1, skip the next st) twice, dc3tog over the last 3 sts, turn.

ROW 3 Ch1, make 1sc in each st and in every ch-1 sp to the end. Fasten off.

TO WORK THE PATTERN
Repeat Rows 2 and 3 using yarn C.

Chevron Bobble Zigzags

Bobbles created from clusters of double crochet stitches add texture to a series of single crochet zigzag stripes. Each colored stripe consists of two rows of single crochet, but you can make the stripes wider if you wish or add more bobbles at the points in the zigzags.

MATERIALS

Cascade Ultra Pima Fine (100% pima cotton; 1.75 oz/50 g; 136.5 yds /125 m)

Deep coral 3767 (yarn A)
Taupe 3759 (yarn B)
Natural 3718 (yarn C)
Coral 3752 (yarn D)
Spring Green 3762 (yarn E)

HOOK SIZE

G-6 (4 mm) crochet hook

SKILL LEVEL

Intermediate

GAUGE

28sc in pattern x 8 rows = 4 in. (10 cm) square

FINISHED SIZE

5.25 x 5.25 in. (13 x 13 cm)

INSTRUCTIONS

Work a chain of a multiple of 16 sts, plus 2 for the Foundation Row.

FOUNDATION ROW Using yarn A, make 2sc in the 2nd ch from the hook, * 1sc in each of the next 7 ch, skip the next ch, make 1sc in each of the next 7 chs, make 3sc in the next ch; repeat from *, ending with 2sc in the last ch, turn.

ROW 1 Ch1, make 2sc in the first st, * 1sc in each of the next 7 sts, skip the next 2 sts, make 1sc in each of the next 7 sts, make 3sc in the next st; repeat from *, ending with 2sc in the last st, turn.

ROW 2 Ch1, make 2sc in the first st, * 1sc in each of the next 3 sts, MB, make 1sc in each of the next 3 sts, skip the next 2 sts, make 1sc in each of the next 3 sts, MB, make 1sc in each of the next 3 sts, make 3sc in the next st; repeat from *, ending with 2sc in the last st. Fasten off and change to yarn B, turn.

ROW 3 Repeat Row 1.

ROW 4 Repeat Row 1; fasten off yarn and change to yarn C.

TO WORK THE PATTERN

Repeat Rows 1–4 and change colors every 2 rows as follows:
Rows 5 and 6: Yarn C.
Rows 7 and 8: Yarn D.
Rows 9 and 10: Yarn E.
Rows 11 and 12: Yarn A.
Rows 13 and 14: Yarn B.
Rows 15 and 16: Yarn C.
Rows 17 and 18: Yarn D.
Rows 19 and 20: Yarn E.

Gentle Fan Zigzags

Exaggerated crochet fans linked with sections of chain stitch create a graphic zigzag lace. For a dramatic look, enhance the visual appeal by working the shells in stripes of bright red, yellow, and pink, with a cool white contrasting yarn.

MATERIALS

Cascade Ultra Pima Fine
(100% pima cotton; 1.75 oz/50 g;
136.5 yds /125 m)

Natural 3718 (yarn A)
Lipstick Red 3755 (yarn B)
Deep Coral 3767 (yarn C)
Buttercup 3748 (yarn D)

HOOK SIZE

G-6 (4 mm) crochet hook

SKILL LEVEL

Intermediate

GAUGE

1.5 fans x 9 rows = 4 in. (10 cm)
square

FINISHED SIZE

5.5 x 4 in. (14 x 10 cm)

INSTRUCTIONS

Work a chain of a multiple of 13 sts, plus 4 for the Foundation Row.

FOUNDATION ROW Using yarn A, make 1dc into the 4th ch from the hook (counts as 2dc), make 1dc into each of the next 3 ch, (dc2tog over the next 2 ch) 3 times, make 1dc into each of the next 3 ch, * 3dc into the next ch, make 1dc into each of the next 3 ch, (dc2tog over the next 2 ch) 3 times, make 1dc into each of the next 3 ch, repeat from * to the last ch, make 2dc in the last ch. Fasten off yarn A and change to yarn B, turn.

ROW 1 Ch3, make 2dc into the first st (counts as 3dc), ch2, skip the next 4dc, make 1sc into the next st, ch4, skip the next st, make 1sc into the next st, ch2, * skip the next 4dc, make 5dc into the next st, ch2, skip the next 4 sts, make 1sc into the next st, ch4, skip the next st, make 1sc into the next st, ch2; repeat from * to the last 4 sts, skip the last 4 sts, make 3dc into the top of the t-ch. Fasten off yarn B and change to yarn C, turn.

ROW 2 Ch3, make 1dc into the first st, make 2dc into the next st, make 1dc into the next st, ch2, skip the next ch-2 sp, make 1sc into the next ch-4 sp, ch2, skip the next sc, make 1dc into the first 4 sts,

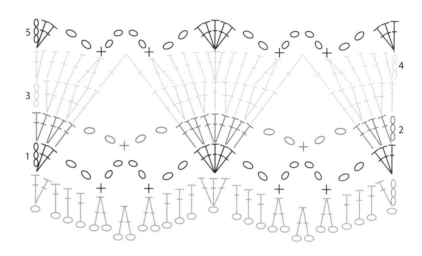

make 2dc into the next st, * 3dc into the next st, make 2dc into the next st, make 1dc into the next st, ch2, skip the next ch-2 sp, make 1sc into the next ch-4 sp, ch2, skip the next sc, make 1dc into the next tr, make 2dc into the next st; repeat from *, ending with 2dc into the top of the t-ch. Fasten off yarn C and change to yarn D, turn.

ROW 3 Ch3, (make 2dc into the next st, 1dc into the next st) twice, skip the next sc, make 1dc into the next dc, * (make 2dc into the next st, 1dc into the next st) 4 times, skip the next sc, make 1dc into the next st; repeat from * to the last 3 sts, make 2dc into the next dc, make 1dc into the next st, make 2dc into the next st,

make 1dc into the top of the t-ch. Fasten off yarn D and change to yarn A, turn.

ROW 4 Ch3, make 1dc into each of the first 4 sts, (dc2tog over the next 2 sts) 3 times, make 1dc into each of the next 3 sts, * 3dc into the next st, make 1dc into each of the next 3 sts, (dc2tog over the next 2 sts) 3 times, make 1dc into each of the next 3 sts; repeat from *, ending with 2dc in the top of the t-ch.

TO WORK THE PATTERN Repeat Rows 1–4 and change colors as follows:
Row 5: Yarn B.
Row 6: Yarn C.
Row 7: Yarn D.
Row 8: Yarn A.

Crochet Essentials

Before you crochet your first motif you will need some yarn, a crochet hook, and a few notions—items such as pins and a tape measure. This section explains how to take your first steps in crochet.

YARNS

Yarns made from plant fibers, such as cotton, linen, and bamboo, are lightweight and breathable. These yarns are usually smooth, which makes it easy to see the stitches as you crochet. Yarns made from animal fibers, like wool, mohair, alpaca, and silk, are warm and absorbent. These yarns are very elastic, making them easy and pleasant to work with. Yarns made from synthetic fibers, including acrylic, nylon, and rayon, are inexpensive, machine-washable, and perfect for blankets and children's wear. Some yarns contain a mixture of fibers. For example, cotton yarn containing synthetic fibers is more elastic and gives a better drape.

The projects in this book are perfect for using up the remnants of yarn in your stash.

HOOKS

Crochet hooks come in standard sizes that are marked on the handle; the sizes are based on the US letter/numbering system or a metric measurement, such as G-6 (4 mm). A pattern will recommend a hook size for a project that is suitable for the yarn weight.

Hooks are available in many styles and materials—such as aluminum, wood, and plastic. Experiment to see which style crochet hook suits you. An ergonomic design is recommended for comfort and flexibility.

When selecting a hook, a general rule is the thicker the yarn, the bigger the hook.

NOTIONS

You won't need to purchase many items for crocheting. Here is a list of the few items that you should have on hand. As with most crafts, it's worthwhile to invest in good quality tools.

SMALL SHARP SCISSORS

Purchase a good pair of scissors. They'll definitely come in handy.

PINS

Purchase sewing pins with round tips so you can see them easily. Have plenty because you will need them when blocking your finished items (see page 140).

STITCH MARKERS

These are very useful for marking the beginning and end of rounds/rows and for marking position details in a pattern.

TAPE MEASURE

This is essential for checking your tension and measurements in a pattern. A small ruler is also a handy tool to have with you, to quickly check the motif measurements.

NEEDLES

These may be called darning needles or tapestry needles. They will have a large eye for threading thicker yarn, and they are used for weaving in threads and sewing pieces of crochet together.

Getting Started

MAKING A SLIP KNOT

Begin by making your first loop (called a slip knot).

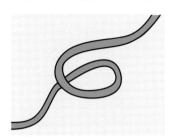 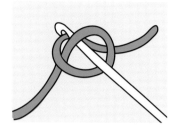 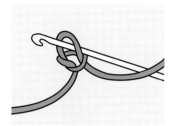 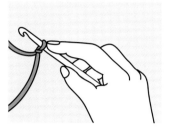

STEP 1 Take your yarn and hold the ball end between the forefinger and thumb of your right hand; hold the tail end in your left hand. Circle the yarn clockwise over the top of the ball end to make a loop.

STEP 2 Insert the hook into the circle, and using it to grab the ball end of the yarn, pull the yarn through. Cross the yarn coming from the right over the yarn coming from the left, to form a circle loop. Pinch your left finger and thumb over the spot where the yarn comes together.

STEP 3 Pinch your left finger and thumb over the spot where the yarn comes together. Pull both ends of the yarn firmly to tighten the knot around the shaft of the hook.

STEP 4 Make sure you leave at least a 4-in. (10-cm) yarn tail for weaving in later. Now you are ready to make your first stitch.

HOLDING THE YARN

I recommend that beginners start with a worsted weight yarn and an H-8 (5 mm) hook. Using a pale colored yarn will make it easier to see your stitches.

HOLDING THE HOOK

It is important to find the right method that works best for you. A comfortable grip means your hands will not cramp and your gauge will be even (see page 135).

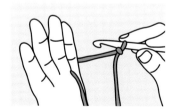 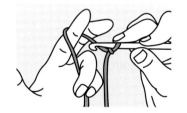 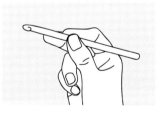 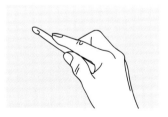

STEP 1 The hand that holds the yarn (left hand for right-handed people, and vice versa) feeds the yarn to your hook and plays a vital role in keeping an even tension in your crochet. Wrap the ball end of yarn around your little finger.

STEP 2 Pass the yarn under the next two fingers and over the top of your forefinger. You can also position the yarn over your middle finger instead—experiment until you find the most comfortable way of making a slip knot that works for you.

HOLD 1 Hold your hook like a pencil with your thumb and forefinger resting on each side of the hook. Make sure the hook is facing toward you, not facing up or down.

HOLD 2 Hold your hook in the palm of your hand like a knife, with your thumb resting on the front of the hook, and your forefinger holding the hook from the other side.

Getting Started continued

MAKING A CHAIN

Once you have your first stitch on the hook, it's time to make a chain (ch). While making your chain, you will get used to holding your yarn and hook and improving your gauge.

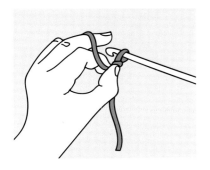

STEP 1 With a slipknot on your hook, move your hook under the yarn in your left hand, grab the yarn (called a "yarn over"), and pull through the loop on the hook. First chain is made.

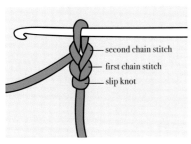

— second chain stitch
— first chain stitch
— slip knot

STEP 2 Repeat this step until you have the required number of chains you need for the pattern. When counting chains, do not count the loop that is on the hook.

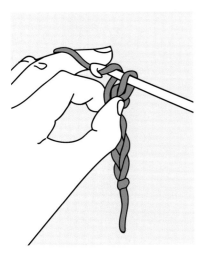

STEP 3 After you have made each chain, move your finger and thumb on the left hand up to pinch your last stitch. So make a chain, pinch, and repeat. After practice, this movement will become easy and almost automatic!

WORKING STITCHES INTO THE CHAIN

Each of these methods works well, just be consistent with the one you choose. Working into the foundation chain can be awkward at first, and it is important to keep the chain from twisting.

Working through the top loop of the chain

From the front, each chain looks like interlocking Vs. Insert the hook from the front of the chain, through the center of one of these 'V-'stitches, and pick up the top loop only.

Working through the back ridge of the chain

On the back of the chain you will see little bumps with ridges. Insert the hook into these bumps to get a different look of your foundation chain.

Working through both loops of the chain

This is the most difficult method, but it gives a firm finish and replicates the way you will crochet into stitches on subsequent rows. To do it, insert the hook under the top two loops from front to back.

Stitches

WORKING A SLIP STITCH

The slip stitch (sl st) is the smallest of all the stitches and is used to join rounds, or as part of the pattern.

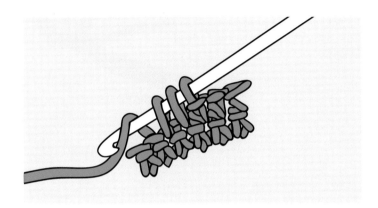

STEP 1 Insert the hook into the indicated stitch, yarn over, and pull the yarn through the stitch, and loop on the hook in one movement.

SINGLE CROCHET

Make your first single crochet (sc) stitch in the second chain from the hook on your foundation chain.

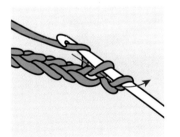

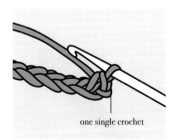

one single crochet

STEP 1 Insert the hook in the stitch indicated in the pattern, yarn over, and pull the yarn through the stitch.

STEP 2 You will now have 2 loops on your hook.

STEP 3 Yarn over and pull the yarn through both loops on the hook.

STEP 4 You have made a single crochet (sc) stitch. When you reach the end of a row/round, you will need to make a turning chain (t-ch) of 1 ch. Turn your work, and insert the hook under the top of the two loops in the first stitch and work 1sc. Continue making single crochets.

Stitches continued

DOUBLE CROCHET

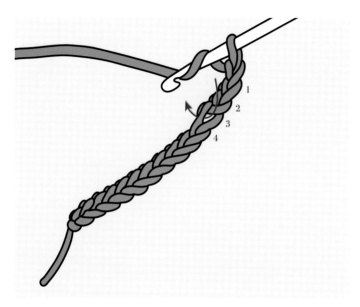

STEP 1 Make your first double crochet stitch (dc) in the fourth chain from the hook on your foundation chain. Yarn over the hook and insert the hook into the stitch indicated in the pattern.

STEP 2 Yarn over again, and pull the yarn through the stitch. You will now have 3 loops on your hook.

STEP 3 Yarn over and pull the yarn through the first 2 loops on the hook.

STEP 4 You will now have 2 loops on your hook.

STEP 5 Yarn over and pull the yarn through the 2 loops on the hook. You have made 1 double crochet stitch.

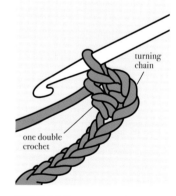

STEP 6 When you reach the end of a row/round, you will need to make a turning chain (t-ch) of 3 chains. Continue making double crochet stitches by inserting your hook under both loops on the top of each stitch from the row below.

HALF DOUBLE CROCHET

STEP 1 Make your first half double crochet (hdc) stitch in the third chain from the hook on your foundation chain.

STEP 2 Yarn over the hook and insert the hook in the stitch indicated in the pattern, yarn over, and pull the yarn through the stitch.

STEP 3 Yarn over again and pull the yarn through all 3 loops on your hook. Half double crochet (hdc) stitch made.

STEP 4 When you reach the end of a row/round, make a turning chain (t-ch) of 2 chains. Continue making half double crochet (hdc) stitches by inserting your hook under both loops on the top of each stitch from the row below.

STEP 5 When you reach the end of a row, you will make your last stitch into the top of the turning chain (t-ch).

TREBLE CROCHET

STEP 1 Make your first treble crochet (tr) stitch into the fifth chain from the hook on your foundation chain.

STEP 2 Yarn over the hook twice and insert the hook into the stitch indicated in the pattern, yarn over again, and pull the yarn through the stitch. You will now have 4 loops on your hook.

STEP 3 Yarn over and pull the yarn through the first 2 loops on the hook. You will now have 3 loops on the hook.

STEP 4 Yarn over and pull through the next 2 loops. You will now have 2 loops on the hook. Yarn over and pull

through the final 2 loops. Treble crochet stitch made.

STEP 5 When you reach the end of a row/round, you will need to make a turning chain (t-ch) of 4 chains. This will bring the first treble crochet (tr) stitch up to the proper height for the next row/round. Make 4 chains (ch4) and turn your work.

STEP 6 Continue making treble (tr) crochet stitches by inserting your hook under 2 loops on the top of each stitch from the row below.

When you reach the end of a row, you will make your last stitch into the top of the turning chain (t-ch).

GAUGE

Gauge—measured by the number of rows and stitches in a 4-in. (10-cm) square—is important because it ensures your finished item is the correct size and uses the amount of yarn stated in the pattern. If your gauge is too tight, the piece will be too small; too loose and it will be too big, and you may not have enough yarn.

The projects in this book are written to be relaxing while making them, so as long as each motif is the same size, you can complete the project. However, we have included gauge so you can check your gauge is correct.

- If your crochet piece is smaller than stated in the pattern, or if it feels stiff, try a larger hook.

- If your piece is too large and the stitches appear to be loose, try a smaller hook.

- For round, square, and triangular motifs, make a complete motif and measure it.

- For crochet worked backward and forward (such as stripe and zigzag patterns), use the yarn and hook size recommended in the pattern to make a gauge square about 6 in. (15 cm) square and use a ruler to measure 4 in. (10 cm) horizontally and vertically in your square. Mark the square with pins. Count the number of stitches, or pattern repeats and rows, between the pins.

- Measure your motifs after blocking (see page 140).

Stitches continued

Stitches are decreased by working two or more together. This is also how clusters, shells, and bobbles are made (see page 139).

DECREASING STITCHES

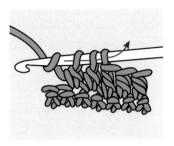

Single crochet: sc2tog
STEP 1 Insert the hook into the first stitch and pull up a loop (2 loops on hook).

STEP 2 Insert the hook into the next stitch and pull up a loop (3 loops on hook).

STEP 3 Yarn over the hook and pull through all 3 loops.

Double crochet: dc2tog
STEP 1 Yarn over, insert the hook into the first stitch, and pull up a loop, yarn over, and pull through 2 loops on the hook. (2 loops on hook)

STEP 2 Yarn over and insert the hook into the next stitch and pull up a loop, yarn over, and pull through 2 loops. (3 loops on hook)

STEP 3 Yarn over and pull through 3 loops.

Double crochet: dc3tog
STEP 1 Yarn over, insert the hook into the first stitch, pull up a loop, yarn over, and pull through 2 loops on the hook. (2 loops on hook)

STEP 2 Yarn over and insert the hook into the next stitch and pull up a loop, yarn over, and pull through 2 loops on the hook, (3 loops on hook)

STEP 3 Yarn over, insert the hook into the next stitch, pull up a loop, yarn over, and pull through the 2 loops. (4 loops on hook)

STEP 4 Yarn over and pull through all 4 loops on the hook. (1 loop on hook)

Treble crochet: tr3tog
Work a treble stitch into first stitch until 2 loops remain on the hook. Work another treble in the next stitch until 3 loops remain on the hook; work another treble in the next stitch until 4 loops remain on the hook. Yarn over and pull through all 4 loops.

Treble crochet: tr2tog
Work a treble stitch in first stitch until 2 loops remain on the hook. Work another treble in the next stitch until 3 loops remain on the hook; yarn over and pull through all 3 loops.

INCREASING STITCHES

Increasing stitches at the end of a row
To increase stitches at the end of the row: work 2 or more sts into the last space or stitch.

Increasing stitches within a row
To increase stitches within a row: work 2 or more sts into the space or stitch designated in the pattern.

Working in the Round

Working in the round always starts with a ring.
Here are two ways to make one.

THE MAGIC RING

Can also be called "magic circle" or "loop". It gives a finished look to your work, and it makes sure there are no holes in the center of your project.

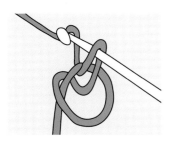

STEP 1 Leaving a 6-8 in. (15-20 cm) tail, make a loop with your yarn. With the thumb and forefinger of your left hand, grasp the join where the yarn overlaps.

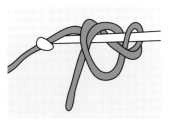

STEP 2 Insert your hook in the circle and pull through the loop; make sure the loop is from the ball end of the yarn.

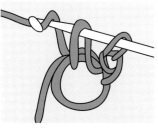

STEP 3 To begin, chain the amount of chains given in the pattern.

STEP4 Work the remaining number of stitches into the loop and over the yarn tail. Join with a slip stitch and pull on the yarn tail to tighten ring.

MAKING A CHAIN RING

Make the number of chains as directed in the pattern. Join with a slip stitch to the first chain made. You are now ready to crochet your first round. You'll work the stitches into the ring and over the chains.

WORKING INTO A SINGLE CHAIN STITCH

Make the chain loose so it is easier to work the stitches into the center space.

TIPS ON WORKING IN THE ROUND

Crocheting a circle is the basis for all circular crochet motifs and many patterns, including hats, cushions, and coasters. Increasing evenly in the round is an important skill, and you will want to end up with a circle that does not curl out or tighten in.

Remember to increase the same number of stitches that you started with in each round:

- For single crochet (sc), work in multiples of 6.
- For half double crochet (hdc), work in multiples of 8.
- For double crochet (dc), work in multiples of 12.

Joining Rounds

JOINING ROUNDS WITH SLIP STITCH

Crochet around the ring as per pattern instructions. After crocheting your last stitch, insert the hook into the top of the first stitch, yarn over, and pull the yarn through both the stitch and loop on the hook.

JOINING ROUNDS WITH AN INVISIBLE NEEDLE JOIN

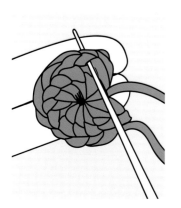

STEP 1 Complete the final stitch for your round/row. Cut the yarn, leaving at least 4-6 in. (10–15 cm) Drop the hook from the loop and pull the tail all the way through the stitch. Thread the yarn tail through your yarn needle.

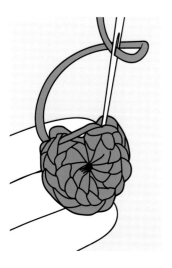

STEP 2 Insert the needle from the front to the back under the top 2 loops of the first complete stitch made to your left. Take your needle and insert it in the back loop only of the last stitch made to your right. Pull through the stitch and weave in the ends.

Working in Rows

It is important to count stitches carefully, and always work into first stitch and last stitch to keep your row even. The pattern may tell you to make your last stitch in the turning chain from the previous row. Putting a stitch marker in the top of the turning chain will help you see the space.

TURNING CHAINS

When you reach the end of a row/round, you will need to make a turning chain (t-ch). This will bring the first stitch up to the proper height for the next row/round. The turning chain is sometimes counted as a stitch, particularly when working trebles and larger stitches. It will say in the pattern whether a turning chain counts as a stitch or not.

The pattern will tell you how many stitches are needed to get your first and turning chain to match the height of the stitches.

- 1 chain for single crochet (sc)
- 2 chains for half double crochet (hdc)
- 3 chains for double crochet (dc)
- 4 chains for treble crochet (tr)

When you reach the end of a row, make your last stitch into the top of the turning chain (t-ch), by inserting your hook into the top of the chains.

WORKING INTO SPACES

Chain spaces are gaps created by making chains between stitches. Sometimes a pattern will ask you to work a specific stitch into a chain space (ch-sp), rather than into a stitch. When instructed to do so, simply insert your hook into the space/gap beneath the chain(s) to make your stitch.

Textured Stitches

CLUSTER

A cluster is made by working incomplete stitches into a single stitch or space and then joining them together to form one stitch. It is worked in the same way as decreasing stitches (see page 136).

BOBBLE

A bobble is made by working incomplete stitches into a single stitch or space and then joining them together to form one stitch.

Make bobble (MB) or dc4tog Yarn over and insert your hook into the stitch/space indicated in the pattern. Yarn over and pull though the st, yarn over and pull through 2 loops on the hook (2 loops on hook). Repeat 3 more times in the same stitch, leaving the last loop of each stitch on the hook; yarn over and pull through all 5 loops to complete stitch.

V-STITCH

To make a V-stitch (1dc, ch1, 1dc in the same space), work 1 double crochet, chain 1, 1 double crochet all in the same stitch/ space.

CHANGING YARN COLORS

Changing colors at the end of a round or row simply means changing yarns at the last yarn over (yo) of the last stitch.

Work the last stitch until there are 2 loops on the hook, yarn over (yo) with the new color, and pull through all the loops to complete the stitch. Make sure to leave at least 6 in. (15 cm) of yarn to weave in later. You are now ready to make the beginning chain in the new color.

If you are crocheting stitches that are close together, you can carry your yarn end underneath the first few stitches and snip the ends later.

Edgings

SINGLE CROCHET

A single crochet (sc) edging is often used as the base row for a decorative edging. It also makes a neat edging for framing your crochet. The pattern will instruct you to make single crochet stitches on the straight edges of your piece and make 2 or 3 single crochet stitches in the corner. Ending with the invisible needle join technique (see page 138) makes a neat finish.

CRAB STITCH (REVERSE SINGLE CROCHET)

Work a row of single crochet (sc) but do not turn your work. Crab stitch is worked from left to right. Insert hook into the second to last stitch completed. Yarn over, and pull through the stitch. Yarn over, and pull through the two loops on the hook. Insert hook into next stitch to the right and repeat. Continue across the row.

PICOT

A picot stitch edging gives a delicate finish to your crochet. It is made with single crochet stitches and chains. After making your first single crochet stitch, make 3 chains (or the number of chains in the pattern instructions) and slip stitch into the first chain. One picot made. Make a single crochet in the next stitch. You can continue with a picot in every second stitch, or you can work more single crochet stitches between every picot.

Finishing your Work

SECURING AND WEAVING IN ENDS

This is very important for a neat, professional finish. It is a good idea to weave in your ends as often as possible while making your project, rather than facing a huge task on completion. Make sure you leave a yarn tail of at least 6–8 in. (15–20 cm) to weave in. Thread a large tapestry needle with your yarn end thread, and working on the wrong side, weave through the loops for at least 3 in. (7.5 cm), then weave again in the opposite direction. Cut off the excess yarn.

BLOCKING AND IRONING

Blocking turns your crochet into a finished item. That crumpled, uneven triangle will be transformed into a neat, even piece by magic! For synthetic manmade fibers, like acrylic, pin your crochet to the correct size on a blocking mat or ironing board. Spray with cold water and let dry. For natural fibers, like wool and cotton, you can pin as above and hold a steam iron about 1–2 in. (2.5–5cm) over your crochet piece. Let cool completely and remove the pins. This method works well with all the motifs in this book.

Joining Blocks

SEWING

Mattress Stitch This gives a neat, invisible seam that is not bulky. With right sides facing up, place the motifs to be joined on a flat surface. Thread your needle with matching yarn and insert the needle into the bottom loops of one piece, then repeat in the opposite piece. Continue stitching between motifs until the end, gently tightening the yarn as you go, and fasten off.

Back Stitch A strong seam for joining motifs. Thread your needle with matching yarn, and hold the right sides of motifs together. Insert the needle from the front to the back through both motifs, and secure it with another stitch. Continue by inserting the needle into the same hole as the last stitch and back up to the front again about a ¼ in. (5 mm) further on. Continue stitching until the seam is finished.

Over Sewing (Whipstich) A quick method of stitching motifs together. Thread your tapestry needle with matching yarn. Place the right sides together and pin, if necessary, so the stitches are matched and lined up. Insert the needle through both loops of the motifs and continue stitching through each loop on one side and the adjacent loop on the other side until the end. Fasten off.

CROCHETING

Single Crochet This method of joining, if worked from the front, creates a decorative ridge on your crochet. You can crochet through just one loop of each motif, or through both loops. Hold both pieces to be joined together, with either the right or wrong sides together, depending what your pattern calls for. Insert the hook through the first stitch of both pieces; ch1 and work 1sc in the same stitch. Insert the hook in the next stitch of both pieces and make 1sc. Continue until both pieces are joined, making sure to match your stitches on both sides.

Slip Stitch A similar method to the single crochet seam, but using a slip stitch instead. You can make the join to either the front or the back of the project. Each gives a different look. Hold both pieces to be joined together, right or wrong sides together, depending on what your pattern calls for. Insert the hook into the first stitch of both pieces to be joined, yarn over, and pull through the two layers and loop on the hook. Continue until the seam is made.

Following a Pattern

UNDERSTANDING WRITTEN INSTRUCTIONS

Crochet patterns are a concise step-by-step guide to creating your crochet piece. They may be intimidating at first (like learning a new language!), but once you familiarize yourself with the abbreviations used, everything will fall into place. When starting out, work a few beginner patterns before progressing to the next level.

Read the abbreviations below and the pattern before you begin. The patterns will be written for rounds (squares, circles, triangles), or in rows (stripe, zigzag). Brackets will give you a set of stitch instructions to follow and a pair of asterisks * to * will also include instructions within them, as well as how many repeats before you move on to the next part of the pattern.

Remember to take it slowly. If you do, you will find that patterns are not as difficult as they seem.

ABBREVIATIONS

[]	work instructions within brackets for as many times as directed	CC	contrasting color	dc5tog	double crochet 5 stitches together	st(s)	stitches
		ch	chain stitch			t-ch	turning chain
()	work instructions within brackets for as many times as directed	ch-	refers to chain or space previously made (i.e. ch-1 space)	g	gram	tog	together
				hdc	half double crochet	tr	treble crochet
		ch-sp	chain space	m	meter(s)	tr2tog	treble crochet 2 stitches together
*	repeat the instructions following the single asterisk as directed	cl	cluster	MB	make bobble (dc4tog)	tr3tog	treble crochet 3 stitches together
		cm	centimeter(s)	oz	ounce(s)		
**	repeat the instructions between the asterisks as many times as directed	dc	double crochet	rnd(s)	round(s)	tr4tog	treble crochet 4 stitches together
		dc2tog	double crochet 2 stitches together	RS	right side	V-st	V stitch
		dc3tog	double crochet 3 stitches together	sc	single crochet	WS	wrong side
in.	inches	dc4tog	double crochet 4 stitches together	sc2tog	single crochet 2 stitches together	yd(s)	yards
beg	beginning			sk	skip	yo	yarn over
bet	between			sl st	slip stitch	yoh	yarn over hook

Following a Pattern

READING A CHART

Just as written crochet instructions guide you step-by-step through a pattern, crochet charts also provide a visual guide. They contain a universal language that provides an alternative way to reading patterns. Each symbol represents a pattern stitch, and by familiarizing yourself with these symbols, you will see that all the pattern information is packed into this visual picture.

When working in rows, you start from the bottom up.

When working in rounds, you will start in the center and work your rounds outward. Each round will be numbered, and the directions given, and charts, are worked counter clockwise.

Learning to read crochet charts gives you a huge advantage in your crochet journey. Start with a familiar pattern (like a Granny Square), and with practice, you will be reading charts with ease.

LEGEND TO THE CHARTS IN THIS BOOK

These are the symbols used in the charts in this book. They are quick to memorize and will enable you to read any crochet chart.

⬯	Chain (ch)
●	slip stitch (sl st)
+	single crochet (sc)
T	half double crochet (hdc)
double crochet symbol	double crochet (dc)
treble crochet symbol	treble crochet (tr)
A	dc2tog
dc3tog symbol	dc3tog
shell symbol	5-dc shell
tr3tog symbol	tr3tog
cluster symbol	dc3tog cluster
bobble symbol	bobble (dc4tog)

Index

Acknowledgments

I would like to thank the staff at Toucan Books for their huge support, especially Ellen Dupont and Sarah Bloxham (who had faith in me), Julie Brooke who held my hand, Leah Germann for her design skills, Bernard Chau for creating the pattern charts, Shahid Mahmood for the artworks and Mark Winwood and Andy Crawford for their photography.

On a personal level, my lovely husband Sean who puts up with my crochet obsession; my always-supportive sons Luke and Ciaran; sister Margaret; and Annie. A big thank you, too, to the all the wonderful ladies in our crochet community in Tramore who have given encouragement and support.

The publishers would like to thank Cascade Yarns (www.cascadeyarns.co.uk) for supplying yarns for the motifs and many of the projects in this book.

Resources

YARNS

Cascade Yarns
www.cascadeyarns.com

Rico Design
www.rico-design.de

Scheepjeswol
www.scheepjeswol.com

Sirdar
www.sirdar.co.uk

Tivoli Yarns
www.tivolispinners.com

New York

An Imprint of Sterling Publishing Co., Inc.
1166 Avenue of the Americas
New York, NY 10036

LARK CRAFTS and the distinctive Lark logo are registered trademarks of Sterling Publishing Co., Inc.

ISBN 978-1-4547-1019-6

Distributed in Canada by Sterling Publishing Co., Inc.
c/o Canadian Manda Group, 664 Annette Street
Toronto, Ontario, M6S 2C8 Canada

For information about custom editions, special sales, and premium and corporate purchases, please contact Sterling Special Sales at 800-805-5489 or specialsales@sterlingpublishing.com.

Manufactured in China

2 4 6 8 10 9 7 5 3 1

www.sterlingpublishing.com
www.larkcrafts.com

Project Editor: Julie Brooke
Proofreader: Marion Dent
Americanizer: Cassie Armstrong
Designer: Leah Germann
Photographs by Mark Winwood (projects) and Andy Crawford (motifs)
Crochet charts by Bernard Chau
Artwork by Shahid Mahmood